Francis Dumaurier

Born and raised in the neighbourhood of Montmartre in Paris, Francis wrote his Masters thesis on Jack Kerouac at the University of Paris X before going on the road to travel and see the world. After a year in the Amazon jungle of Colombia as a rainforest safari guide, he spent five years in Rio de Janeiro working in the travel and tourism industries.

Moving to New York City, he began working in the entertainment industry, first as a host and producer of primetime daily programs on Manhattan Cable TV, and then as an actor in films, TV and voice-overs. Since then he has also hosted and produced "The Wine CD" as a Compagnon des Vins de Bordeaux with a group of other wine specialists.

Fluent in four languages and well versed in the rites of Freemasonry, Francis also loves to play rock'n'roll music on his Stratocaster guitar and Marshall amp.

www.francisdumaurier.com

First published in the UK in 2023 by Supernova, an imprint of Aurora Metro Publications Ltd. 80 Hill Rise, Richmond, TW10 6UB
www.aurorametro.com   info@aurorametro.com
T: @aurorametro Instagram: @aurora_metro
Giorgio Gomelsky 'For Your Love' copyright © 2023 Francis Dumaurier
Foreword copyright © 2023 Rick Rees
Cover design copyright © 2023 Aurora Metro Publications
Cover Photo © 2023 Shawn Brackbill
Editor: Cheryl Robson
Printed on paper which has been sustainably resourced.
ISBNs:
978-1-913641-34-4 (print)
978-1-913641-35-1 (ebook)

GIORGIO GOMELSKY
'FOR YOUR LOVE'

A biography by

FRANCIS DUMAURIER

with a foreword by
RICK REES

SUPERNOVA BOOKS

To my wife, Lilian,
who was a great friend of Giorgio's.

Parce que c'était lui, parce que c'était moi
[Because it was him, because it was me]

– Michel de Montaigne, *Les Essais*, 1580

Acknowledgments
Thanks to: Nicole Devilaine, Ronald Mehu (Bird), Bob Gruen, Jesse Malin, Madeleine Carr, Brian Godding, Larry Birnbaum, Raul Gonzalez, David Godlis, Roman Iwasiwka, Daniel Lesueur, Rick Rees, Brad Schreiber, Jean-Marc Gagnioud, Bradley Rim, Amy Madden, Jon Sadleir, Donatella Guichard Gomelsky, Cheryl Robson, and Lilian Dumaurier.

Pull Quotes
Thanks to Jon Sadleir for the inclusion of material from his video interviews with Gomelsky.

Photo Credits
Giorgio Gomelsky in his studio, Shawn Brackbill ©2014, Giorgio Gomelsky on his bicycle in Manhattan at night, David Godlis ©GODLIS, Birthday party for Julie Driscoll, Madeleine Carr ©1967, Brian Godding at the BBC, Brian Godding ©1969, Portrait of Bill Laswell at Moers Festival, Michael Hoefner ©2006, The Volcanos at Max's Kansas City, George Bezusko ©1982, Roman Iwasiwka, Peter Iwasiwka ©2016, Portrait of Jesse Malin and Giorgio Gomelsky, Bob Gruen ©2005, Larry Birnbaum's selfie, Larry Birnbaum ©2017, Portrait of Giorgio Gomelsky on a wall, Bob Gruen ©2015, Giorgio and Janice Daley, Bob Gruen ©2009, Portrait of Giorgio Gomelsky and Bob Gruen, Bob Gruen ©2006, Portrait of Jesse Malin, Gillian Stoll ©2015, Portrait of Brad Rim, Brad Rim ©1982, Portrait of Amy Madden, Leland Bobbé ©2016, Raul Gonzalez at the memorial ceremony, Raul Gonzalez ©2016, Raul Gonzalez sitting with guitar, Raul Gonzalez ©2015. All the other photographs are either publicity photos, in the public domain, or from the personal archives of Francis Dumaurier.

Giorgio Gomelsky

1934 – 2016

"People have said to me "Write a book, write a book, write a book!" and I've thought about it... the things behind the scenes interest me more than biographical crap. Being a witness is important."

– GOMELSKY

"When I got to London, the pubs closed at 9:30... I came from Paris to London. And guys were up all f***ing night, talking, smoking, and arguing till seven in the morning. No problem. And there, 9:30! Nothing. Nowhere to go."
– GOMELSKY

Giorgio Gomelsky backstage at Wembley with Mick Jagger and Charlie Watts c.1964

CONTENTS

FOREWORD

Rick Rees

Giorgio Gomelsky was the first manager for the Rolling Stones. If you know his name at all, this is probably the one fact that you associate with him, even though their time together was brief. If you happen to know a bit more about Gomelsky, it's likely to be that he next managed the Yardbirds and helped them produce their biggest hits. Or maybe it's that he produced the first solo album *Extrapolation* by John McLaughlin. Or did some of the first recordings with Soft Machine ... or helped Daevid Allen and Gong do their early tours and recordings ... and Magma ... and Bill Laswell's band Material. And on and on. Yet, in spite of this impressive resumé, of which I've just barely scratched the surface, few people know his name. A few years ago, I was among the ignorant, even though the name Giorgio Gomelsky had been staring me down in my record collection for decades.

Meet Francis Dumaurier. He encountered Gomelsky in New York in the early 1980s and they became close personal friends in the decades that followed. By the time they met, most of Gomelsky's legendary stories were behind him. Over the years he would share many of them with Francis. When Gomelsky died in 2016, without making progress on his autobiography, Francis decided to create a memoir of his friendship with Giorgio. And here it is. What started out as a personal life story ended up becoming a personal one-man crusade to get the name Giorgio Gomelsky enshrined into the Rock and Roll Hall of Fame.

Francis is a French expat who moved to New York in the late 1970s. After meeting Gomelsky, the two shared many a romp together in New York City. These stories are not only penetrating and touching, but for me, who never met the man, they were a way to get to know him, not just as a band manager and record producer that had been interviewed many times over the years, but as a person.

About a year after Gomelsky passed away, I developed an obsession about him that would put me on a collision course with Francis. While reading a book about a favourite band of mine from the prog era of the early 1970s, I came across a quote by their recording engineer. He said that after his prog band albums, he did some recording with another band that I also loved. It was a few years later, on another continent, and in a completely different genre consisting of a tight-knit group of artists in New York City forming bands in a post-punk landscape that had rejected prog rock long ago. How could these two disparate worlds have connected? Who could do such a thing? I had to know more, which soon led me to the name Giorgio Gomelsky.

A few hours on the internet produced a mind-boggling list of band names that Gomelsky had worked with. Almost every one of them was in my record collection. It seemed to me that a person this influential must already have a biography written about them. I found none. My obsession grew. I read dozens of interviews spanning decades. I found a couple of books with maybe a chapter about Giorgio. Eventually, I did find this book that you're reading now; except that it was only available in French. I don't speak

French. I moved on, continuing my search elsewhere. The more I discovered about Giorgio, the more I kept coming back to this French book. How could I read this book?

I decided to contact the author. Hoping that he spoke English, I sent him an email. His response was quick. It read something like this: "Who the hell are you?" He used a few more words and was much more diplomatic, but that's what I read. My assumption that this French author lived in France was completely wrong. He was living in New York City and had been for decades. Like most New Yorkers he's suspicious of everyone, until he gets to know you, of course.

We corresponded a bit over the next few months. By then I'd bounced the name Giorgio Gomelsky off my many musician friends and acquaintances. I live on the west coast of America in San Francisco. Like me, no one from the west coast knew the name. Only my New York friends had heard of him. Some had even worked with him and knew him quite well. They agreed that there should be a biography written about the man. Well, I might just know where to find one. I made plans to visit one of my New York friends. I let Francis know. Could we meet?

I called Francis from my friend's place in Brooklyn. We set a time to meet. He lives in Manhattan, so I'll just go to his apartment at the agreed upon time, right? Wrong. He instructs me to go to Columbus Circle and meet him at the base of the statue there. Wow. My visits to New York are always interesting, but this time it's turning into something out of a spy novel. Is his Gomelsky book some kind of contraband in the USA? Is that why it's only available in French? We don't even know what each other look like. I think I sent him my picture after we hung up.

Of course, we had no trouble finding each other. I'll never forget the giant smile he greeted me with. It was a swelteringly hot summer day in NYC. He ushered me into

Central Park, and we started talking about Gomelsky. I had a lot of questions for Francis and not a lot of time to ask them. No matter. All I had to do was listen. We sat on a shaded bench in Strawberry Fields. In the background were tourists listening to street musicians play Beatles songs. The stories started flowing. Should I take notes? Should I start recording this? I just took it in as much as I could. I'm not very good at living in the moment. On this hot day, listening to Francis, I don't think I had any choice.

By the end of our meeting, the only thing I could think of was getting Francis's book published in English. And soon. So, I could read it. It would be a long process involving many people, but here we are.

The influence of Giorgio Gomelsky cannot be overstated. His connections in the music world were so vast and varied that no one person, not even a close friend like Francis, is aware of them all. One person who worked with him said he was "the vibe master." He brought the right people together at the right time and made things happen. And judging by what happened with me and Francis, I'd say he's still doing it.

Rick Rees 2022

1. WAITING FOR GIORGIO

"Music is a tool for revolution."
– GOMELSKY

Back in 2011, when I was writing my autobiography, *Expat New York*,[1] it became obvious that my passions for travelling and rock music have been the two main threads of my life.

My father was an officer in the French army during and after World War II, and moving from one place to another in France, Germany, and Morocco was the normal thing to do until I turned ten, when we finally settled in a bourgeois building located at Place Jules Joffrin, where the city hall of the 18th arrondissement of Paris is also located.

My closest friend at the local primary school introduced me to Bill Haley's "Rock Around the Clock" in 1957, and some of the altar boys at the Catholic church of Notre Dame de Clignancourt played instrumentals made popular by the Shadows, a famous English band of the early 60s. One of these young musicians introduced me to the music of Chuck Berry and Bo Diddley in 1962, and my musical passion took off.

My high school, Lycée Condorcet, was located on Rue du Havre, close to Gare Saint Lazare, and after school I used to go to the second floor of the Printemps department store. I spent hours listening to all the latest rock 'n' roll records. The store began importing records from England during the winter of 1964, and this was how I discovered

1. Available to download for free in French at http://xpatny.free.fr,

the Rolling Stones and all the other great bands that came to us from England after the Beatles.

I would ask the English girls who walked by to help me understand the lyrics of the records I was playing, and one of them even had enough patience to write down the complete lyrics of Chuck Berry's "Promised Land," which I listened to endlessly on the store's tiny speakers.

A friendly young salesman sold electric guitars and amplifiers at a nearby stand. He was also a member of an instrumental band, and he taught me some basic chords and rhythms. I was soon playing blues on guitar as well as the harmonica. When Bob Dylan traded his acoustic for an electric guitar to the dismay of folk purists, naturally I became a huge fan.

Every once in a while, the store promoted special products, for example, wigs styled in a Beatles mop-top hairdo. It also had promotional events with famous French singers like Pierre Perret, but on a surprising day in November 1964, the Beach Boys came to sign autographs and promote the concert they were giving at the Olympia music hall that same night. The store manager asked me if I would agree to act as their translator, since nobody spoke English on the floor, and I accepted with pleasure. I was already familiar with their music – thanks to the hit "I Get Around," which I had discovered in England a few months earlier – and I arrived on time wondering how this adventure was going to turn out.

I found myself with the original group: the brothers Brian, Carl, and Dennis Wilson, their cousin Mike Love, and their friend Al Jardine. I translated what I could on the fly and collected their autographs. It was their last tour with Brian, who had decided to stop travelling and to stay in Los Angeles, where he could better focus on writing songs and producing recording sessions in the studio.

Autographs of the original Beach Boys band
members in Paris on November 18, 1964

Dennis was restless and could not stay in one place – he disappeared quickly – but the others stayed and flirted with the girls. Brian asked me to take him to the perfume area as he wanted to buy something special for his future wife. I was 17 and this was my day in heaven.

To thank me, the store manager gave me two tickets for their evening concert on November 18, 1964, at L'Olympia. It was my very first concert and I had royal seats. Some girls were screaming out in English, others were flocking to the stage, and it was sheer pandemonium. I could not believe my eyes and ears, but it was an amazing experience which I wanted to repeat again.

As I walked by L'Olympia on February 7, 1965, I noticed

| OLYMPIA |

LAISSEZ-PASSER

M ....

valable UNIQUEMENT pour l'accès aux coulisses
et aux loges.

DIMANCHE   ►7 FEV. 1965

La direction,   Mr BORIS

Ce laissez-passer est strictement personnel et ne donne aucun droit à
pénétrer dans la salle, ni sur le plateau, ni de se faire accompagner.
Il peut être retiré à tout moment.

CH. MAILLARD, PUB.

Backstage pass for Chuck Berry's first concert in France at the Olympia
music hall on February 7, 1965

the stage entrance. The VIPs who had just seen Chuck
Berry's first concert in France were coming out, and one
of them looked at me and giving me his backstage pass, he
said, "Take this and enjoy!" I knew that it would allow me to
sneak in through that door for the evening concert.

Although I was nervous about getting caught, I walked
in confidently and arrived backstage just as Ronnie Bird
was leaving the stage in a sweat. Ronnie was one of the
first French rock stars to adapt the English songs with
French lyrics and he dressed like a "mod" rocker. I'd never
have guessed that 15 years later, Ronnie and I would strike
up a friendship in New York that would last for more than
35 years.

Ronnie's musicians stayed on stage, as they were the
backup musicians for Chuck Berry, and I tried to make
myself invisible backstage, watching by the side of the
curtain. Nobody stopped me and I couldn't believe my luck.
When Chuck left the stage, I followed him to his dressing
room, where I met another French rock star, Eddy Mitchell,

with whom I had a brief but very pleasant conversation.

Outside L'Olympia, a large group of fans gathered in the middle of the Boulevard des Capucines and yelled, "Chuck Berry for president! Chuck Berry for president!" When I got back home, my father yelled at me for not calling to let him know that I would be so late. I went straight to bed and fell asleep, exhausted but happy.

Thanks to my newfound method of getting in backstage at the Olympia, I went on to enjoy free concerts by the Rolling Stones in 1965 and 1966, and also James Brown, the Kinks, Roy Orbison, the Nice, Barry McGuire, Bo Diddley, the Walker Brothers, Them, and later, Frank Zappa and the Mothers of Invention.

Since I had a membership at the Locomotive Club, I used to go there on Sunday afternoons and saw a lot of great 60s artists such as the Pretty Things, Gene Vincent, the Moody Blues, Tom Jones, and the Zombies. Another memorable Paris concert was on June 20, 1965, when I saw the Yardbirds open for the Beatles at the Palais des Sports.

It wasn't long before I ventured across the channel to England, where I saw the Who, the Troggs, and the Animals – and this was also where I bought most of my records.

I visited the United States for the first time, landing at JFK airport, on August 10, 1969. I had an incredible experience on my first weekend there at the Woodstock Festival. Then six weeks later, on September 13 and 14, I found myself at the Big Sur Folk Festival located on the coast between San Francisco and Los Angeles. Another notorious music festival from that time which I attended was the Altamont Speedway Free Festival on December 6 where the Rolling Stones performed. The unfortunate events which occurred at Altamont were very well documented in the movie *Gimme Shelter*.

Tickets and program for the Woodstock Music and Art Fair
in August 1969

Ticket for the Big Sur Folk Festival on September 13, 1969
and posters for the Fillmore West Concert Hall

I was privileged to see most of the incredible bands of the late 60s because I spent ten months living in San Francisco. I went to the weekly concerts at the Fillmore West and was able to see Johnny Winter, the Grateful Dead, Jefferson Airplane, Albert King, the Kinks, Delaney and Bonnie with Eric Clapton and Dave Mason, Fleetwood Mac, Sha Na Na, Santana, Country Joe and the Fish, the Byrds, Steve Miller, John Paul Hammond, and Quicksilver Messenger Service.

Although the Fillmore West could accommodate hundreds of people, the promoter Bill Graham used the Winterland Ballroom for his famous concerts as it had a capacity audience of 5,400 people. As progressive rock bands began to offer more spectacular shows, they moved into bigger venues like the Winterland too. That was where I saw Led Zeppelin and the Doors. When the Grateful Dead were jailed for drugs in New Orleans on January 31, 1970, a concert was immediately organized with local bands at the Winterland. The cost was three dollars per person to bail the Dead out of jail, and all the musicians and crew members offered their services for free.

KSAN, the popular local rock station, made a few announcements, and that night I gathered with thousands of other rock fans to see It's a Beautiful Day, Quicksilver Messenger Service with Nicky Hopkins, Santana, and Jefferson Airplane all on the same bill; the musicians of the Grateful Dead were released the next day.

The Family Dog was a club run by Chet Helms on the Great Highway. Chet was the one who had brought Janis Joplin to San Francisco from Texas, where he knew her as a teenager. His club was as famous as the Fillmore West, even if it was smaller and less crowded. When I saw them there, the Grateful Dead and Jefferson Airplane shared the bill, and the concert ended with musicians of both bands jamming together on stage into the early hours. They only stopped when somebody cut the power off at sunrise. Altogether I was lucky to be able to see the Grateful Dead and Jefferson Airplane over a dozen times.

When I returned to Paris in April 1970 to write my master's thesis on Jack Kerouac and the Beat Generation, I knew I was not going to stay there. I had already been a student at the University of Paris X Nanterre since 1967, where I witnessed the student riots of May 1968, and I was no longer interested in that kind of political activism. I had the urge to travel around the world and discover new horizons.

Although I didn't travel as much as I'd planned, I did spend a year in the Amazon rainforest in Colombia as a safari guide, followed by five years working in the travel business in Rio de Janeiro in Brazil. Tiring of the challenges of South America, my beautiful American wife, Irene, and I decided to return to New York City in 1977.

***

It was a few years later, in January 1981, that I first met Giorgio Gomelsky. It seemed quite unbelievable for me to find myself in the same room with the first manager of the Rolling Stones, the first manager and producer of the Yardbirds, the person who introduced the Beatles to the Stones, and much more. And who was it who actually took me to meet Giorgio at his house? Of course, it was Ronald Mehu, aka Ronnie Bird, the very same singer I had loved back in the early days of the French rock scene.

Since arriving in New York I had become involved with cable television, which was a new technology that was expanding at the time. I had met Ronnie a few months earlier in the New York offices of French Broadcasting, for which I had produced a large transatlantic live news event.

As fate would have it, the director of that office was Nicole Devilaine, a close friend of Giorgio's who asked Ronnie to introduce me to him. Giorgio was always keen to understand emerging technologies and he wanted to know more about my experience in cable television, as I was producing my own programs in 1980.

This chance meeting would lead to a friendship with Giorgio which would last for more than 30 years. Our closest period was between 1983 and 1996.

Thanks to *Expat New York*, the illustrated version of my autobiography in French, Daniel Lesueur, the editor of *Camion Blanc*, asked me if I would agree to give Jacques Leblanc – the publisher of *Juke Box Magazine*, (a French monthly specializing in 60s' rock) – the rights to reproduce excerpts of my musical adventures, and I accepted with pleasure.

I stayed in touch with Daniel and Jacques, most particularly with Daniel, who is an avid collector of bootleg records. However, my own experience with bootleg records was short-lived. When I returned to Paris from California in April of 1970, I had offered the manager of the Discobole (a record store near Gare Saint Lazare) to import one hundred copies of *Great White Wonder*, the first significant bootleg ever, which featured a collection of Bob Dylan recordings by himself and with the Band.

When the boxes finally arrived, the store manager was very impressed, as he had half-expected my offer to be nothing more than hot air. He placed the records in a highly visible spot in his store and agreed to consider buying copies of *Stealin,' A Thousand Miles Behind*, and *John Birch Society Blues* – also bootlegs of Bob Dylan – as well as *Live'r Than You'll Ever Be*, which would become *Get Yer Ya-Ya's Out!* by the Rolling Stones, and *Get Back*, which would become *Let It Be* by the Beatles, both of them due out a year later.

The Great White Wonder, first two Bob Dylan bootleg original releases

The next day, however, I received a call from the store manager, who informed me that he now had a big problem. The sales representative from Columbia Records had just been into his store and told him that he had to get rid of the bootleg records immediately, with the threat of never being allowed to sell records from Columbia ever again. As a result he was giving my records away for free to his best customers, and had to now regretfully let me know that our business relationship was over. That was the beginning and the end of my career as a French import-exporter.

Daniel and I therefore enjoyed a unique transatlantic affinity and he asked one of his writers, Didier Delinotte, who was writing a book on Ronnie Bird, to contact me in

April 2017 if he needed additional information on Ronnie for his book.

When Didier's book *Ronnie Bird: Le rock en V. F.* came out, Daniel sent me a copy, which I read in one sitting. I liked the book and sent my positive comments to Daniel, telling him also: "If you decide to do the same about Giorgio Gomelsky someday, I am available for details on his life in New York. I met him during the week of my 34th birthday, when Ronnie took me to his place in January 1981 on the recommendation of Nicole Devilaine, and he passed away on the day of my 69th birthday on January 13, 2016. We were close friends during his midlife crisis of the 80s and stayed in close contact until his declining health forced him into lengthy hospital stays."

On reading my note, Daniel suggested that I write a biography of Giorgio Gomelsky myself, and that he would publish it, which is how this book first came about in French.

The first draft I sent him was not a clinical list of facts, dates, names, and places, and I was a bit afraid that he would reject this personal and unconventional approach. It was more a direct testimony of a long and close friendship that lasted for more than 30 years, with all the subjective baggage that came with it – even though it was also filled with a strong knowledge of the English rock scene of the 60s, with details confirmed by Giorgio during our endless conversations.

After thinking about it, Daniel told me that he was interested, and I set about writing everything I knew as I had lived and felt it. Both Giorgio's humanity and my own came across as simply and purely as I could express them. As I wrote it, I thought it would also be interesting to ask others who knew Giorgio well if they would like to add their own comments, and six of them agreed:

- Madeleine Carr, who worked for Giorgio in London

from 1965 to 1969,

- Brian Godding, songwriter and guitarist of Blossom Toes,

- Larry Birnbaum, music critic and author of *Before Elvis: The Prehistory of Rock 'n' Roll*,

- Jesse Malin, a legend of the New York underground music scene,

- Bob Gruen, rock and roll photographer extraordinaire,

- Raul Gonzalez, a "mariachi punk" musician from Mexico who helped Giorgio run his house during the last eight years of his life and who was the very last friend to see him alive in his hospital bed.

Also, David Gillis gave me permission to use his great black-and-white photo of Giorgio on his bicycle on a Manhattan street at night, the photo that was chosen for the cover of the French edition.

Finally, I received from Roman Iwasiwka – a member of the bands the Volcanos and Surgery, which I managed and who rehearsed in Giorgio's house more than thirty-five years ago, from January 1984 to July 1986 – additional short stories that I am happy to include here.

Naturally, these contributions were sent to me in English, and their authors asked me if I was also going to write an English version of the book. I hesitated to say yes, not only because it was a lot of work, but also because there was no publisher in sight for the English version at the time.

However, since this undertaking was a labour of love, I slowly got used to the idea that I had to write an English version of Giorgio's extraordinary life, a life that had been uniquely productive and that none of us should ever forget.

So, I started typing the translation of this book from French to English with no promise of a financial reward. And then, as a gift from heaven, my friend Larry Birnbaum, whose contribution can be found near the end of this book, agreed to edit my English translation, which proved to be badly in need of qualified supervision.

Then, another gift from heaven came to me unexpectedly. Rick Rees contacted me from San Francisco. He had seen that the French version was on sale on Amazon and, being a fan of Giorgio's productions of the late 70s and early 80s, he wanted to know if an English version was forthcoming. I told him that I was working on it and that I would let him know if and when that would come to pass.

Rick came to visit a friend in Brooklyn in mid-August 2018, and we met at Columbus Circle in Manhattan for a walk in Central Park. We sat for hours on a bench in Strawberry Fields by the iconic mosaic dedicated to John Lennon with the word Imagine in the middle, while tourists were taking pictures and local singers were singing Beatles tunes. I pointed out the location of the terrace on Central Park South by Columbus Circle[2], where Giorgio and I had often spent nights sipping champagne and talking endlessly until sunrise.

Rick told me about a book on the Yardbirds, which Jim McCarty had written and self-published, that he had purchased at a recent Yardbirds concert in San Francisco. I ordered the book and was pleased to see that it validated most of what Giorgio had told me during our conversations over the years. I was also happy to see that Jim's book had been released two months *after* my French version had been published in France by Editions Camion Blanc.

---

2. During our wedding reception, which Lilian and I organized on September 29, 1991, in a French restaurant near Columbus Circle, our friend Jenni Trent passed around a large sheet of parchment paper on which she had glued two photographs of us taken by her during our wedding ceremony at City Hall, and she asked all present to sign it with a personal message of good wishes. Giorgio simply wrote "Fly High!" which perfectly describes how he lived his own life.

Finally, Rick told me about a friend of his, Brad Schreiber, who had written a book about Jimi Hendrix. Brad was also working as a consultant who helped writers like me format their new books in a manner suitable for presentation to American publishers.

Rick generously offered to sponsor Brad's work if I was interested, and I took him up on his offer. Brad has made a great number of suggestions that did improve on the structure and format of this English version of the book.

I'm extremely pleased that my telling of Giorgio's incredible life and journey soon found a publisher in the UK and to be able to finally share this story with readers all over the world.

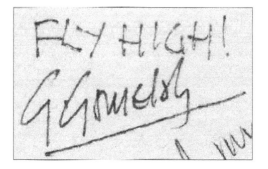

Giorgio Gomelsky on his bike in Manhattan in the 1980s.
Photo: David Godlis©GODLIS

2. GROWING UP IN GEORGIA, IRAN, ITALY, AND SWITZERLAND

"I didn't really have a home country or a mother tongue
or anything like that... it gave me a kind of freedom to
float away... So I was always an anarchist
in that respect."– GOMELSKY

Giorgio Sergio Alessandro Gomelsky was born on February 28, 1934, in Tbilisi, when the country of Georgia was under the Communist thumb of the USSR. His father was a doctor, his mother Éliane (born Wust) was a milliner from Monte Carlo. In 1938, when Joseph Stalin started harassing the middle class, his parents decided to leave Georgia to move to Switzerland, where his father had studied medicine.

However, World War II was about to start, and it became more and more difficult to find a means of transportation and the necessary visas. The family ended up spending time in Syria, Persia (now Iran), and Egypt before getting a boat to Genoa and making their way to the north of Italy, where German soldiers blocked their way to Switzerland.

His early childhood memories were limited to conversations he had with his parents, and he had basically no memento left from the days of Communist oppression in the USSR, at a time when World War II was imminent. He was too young to remember this epic journey well, but one of his earliest memories, which happened to be musical in nature, went back to Persia, where his father had practised medicine and met a lot of people of the region, including a group of five Gypsies whom he had invited to his home at night to play music for the family. The problem was that they only had one violin for five players and that each one had to pass the instrument to the next guy once he had finished his song. From this encounter, Giorgio acquired first-hand knowledge at a very early age that the same instrument could be played with different techniques and produce different sounds once it was in the hands of a different player.

He also told my wife Lilian that his maternal grandmother had been one of the very first female gynaecologists in Georgia, just before World War I, and that could very well have been what inspired his father to study medicine.

Arriving in northern Italy, the village where they were staying was under curfew at 4 p.m., a rule which was enforced by the occupying Nazis as well as by local Italian pro-Nazi groups, and Giorgio was sometimes forced to stay with friends for the night. This was how he discovered American jazz music on a Sunday night when they found a stack of old records and an old gramophone in the attic. One evening, in an act of youthful rebellion, Giorgio and his friends placed the loudspeaker at the window so that the music could be heard in the street, and they were lucky not to get caught.

The group decided to start collecting all the jazz records they could find, and they listened religiously to "Caravan," "Take the 'A' Train," and to a Louis Jordan record in which Jordan sang about chickens, which Giorgio played relentlessly.

Since his father was as much an anti-Fascist as he was an anti-Communist, life was not any easier in Italy than it had been in Georgia, and the family had to wait patiently for the war to end before they could finally move to Switzerland.

With such a nomadic early life, Giorgio would never feel like he belonged to any country.

After this forced sojourn in Italy, he grew up in Switzerland. He went to a Benedictine school in Ascona, near Locarno, where he learned to play boogie-woogie on the church organ, and he tuned in to the army radio station at night, one of the few places you could hear American music in those days. He then studied at the École d'Humanité in the Bernese Oberland town of Hasliberg Goldern. The school was under the direction of Paul Geheeb, a German reformist pedagogue.

When his parents separated and divorced, his mother, Eliane, moved to Paris to work in the workshop of Madame Claude Saint-Cyr, one of the most famous milliners of the day. Eliane had lived in Monaco where her father worked for the Société des Bains de Mer, the company that managed the local casino. As Monaco had long been popular with English tourists, Eliane quickly learned English there and developed a taste for English culture. Claude Saint-Cyr clearly valued Eliane's work in Paris, because she sent Eliane to London to manage her new shop there, working in association with leading fashion designer Norman Hartnell. Consequently, St Cyr's hats were designed for and worn by the Queen and other English royalty, as well as being popular with the upper-class ladies who attended the Ascot horse races.

Knowing his passion for jazz, Eliane regularly sent Giorgio copies of the *Melody Maker* newspaper, which kept him informed of what was happening musically in England and helped him improve his knowledge of the English language at the same time.

At the age of thirteen, Giorgio had a huge argument with his father and would go off hitchhiking or take himself off on bike rides around Europe. This is how he discovered jazz cafés and started living a bohemian life during these strange postwar years.

Back in Zurich as a teenager, he took acting classes, learned to play the drums, wrote articles for an Italian jazz magazine, helped musicians he met to start a band, organized a support group for the appreciation of jazz music in Locarno, took an interest in the art of cinema, and at the age of 19, fathered a son with his girlfriend. They named the boy Sergio.

The collection of jazz records that he and his friends had amassed was impressive, and their taste for jazz was limitless. They rode their bikes to go see jazz concerts in Milan and Paris, and even watched Charlie Parker perform at the Salon du Jazz. At the same time, Giorgio constantly listened to the jazz programs that were broadcast on the Voice of America network, and started a jazz trio in which he played drums with Roland Schramler on bass and Bert Armbruster on piano.

When he tried to produce a jazz festival in Zurich in 1953, City Hall refused to give him the permit. His friends at the Jazz Federation organized a demonstration with him one Sunday in May, and at 4 p.m. sharp, while middle-class families were walking up and down the main avenue, two hundred people got on their knees in the middle of the street, pulled down their pants, and showed their bare arses to the sky. Newspapers reported it the next day, and City Hall belatedly issued the festival permit.

Unfortunately, on the day of the concert, the rain was torrential but at least Giorgio managed to earn some respect from City Hall. He returned to Switzerland in 1964 to produce an outdoor concert in Ascona on a disused airport runway. What he learned organising these events about the value of publicity and the importance of the location would stand him in good stead for his future career in the music industry. Today, Zurich embraces jazz music and has a thriving jazz festival which has been running for more than twenty years.

As a Swiss citizen, Giorgio had to report for military service and he chose to apply to serve in the air force. However, he was not suited to military life, and in spite of his ability to fly Buchner biplanes, he managed to get exempted from military duty by deliberately failing all the tests. This set him free to start travelling abroad and to pursue his devotion to jazz music.

"My mission was to create things that were incredible and it was the exercise of the imagination in terms of what was happening in the relevant music scene. That was what excited me."
– GOMELSKY

Fans hang from the ceiling at the original Crawdaddy Club located at the Station Hotel in Richmond, 1963.
Photo: Jeremy Fletcher

3. SWINGIN' LONDON AND THE CRAWDADDY CLUB

In 1955, at the age of 21, Giorgio managed to arrange financing from an Italian television station to make a documentary on the experimental jazz scene in England. He went to London, and having successfully completed the short film for the Italian TV station, this opened the door to his next cinematic adventure. Next, he produced a longer film shot at the Royal Festival Hall, recording Chris Barber, who was more of a traditional jazz musician, in concert. For the event, Giorgio hired three cameras and shot in black-and-white CinemaScope.

This film was well received and brought Giorgio praise from the critics, which in turn helped him to gain permission from Harold Pendleton of the National Jazz Foundation to film the second National Jazz Festival in 1962, which he did in black and white, this time with four cameras and the most sophisticated sound equipment he could find at the time. He also shot other scenes in a studio, which he edited together with live concert footage to create an interesting documentary.

In order to pay for all this, he convinced the producer Frank Green to finance the project, but unfortunately, Frank failed to find a profitable means of distribution for the film.

For this second film, Giorgio also edited two demos with

Alexis Korner and his Blues Incorporated band, which featured Charlie Watts on drums. But once again, he failed to find a buyer and could not produce other material from his original footage.

After having produced his first films on the London jazz scene, he wrote articles in jazz magazines to earn a few pounds. All in all, Giorgio found that life in London was dreary during the austerity of these postwar years.

Having imported a professional Faema espresso machine from Italy, he opened the Olympic Coffee Bar with a friend (three tables and a few chairs) on King's Road near Sloane Square in the Chelsea neighbourhood of London – coincidentally Chelsea was the name of the New York neighbourhood where he spent the last 38 years of his life. This café attracted young people who came in when local pubs closed at 9 p.m. One of these young people was the then unknown fashion designer Mary Quant, who would later become famous with her invention of the miniskirt.

It was quite possibly as a rebellion against the dull atmosphere of life in postwar London that a new movement started taking shape. New pubs and restaurants opened their doors for a new wave of young people who were starting what became known as "Swingin' London."

Giorgio continued to write his jazz articles, notably for the *Jazz News* magazine, and he coined the acronym BR&B or BRB which stood for British Rhythm and Blues.

Young musicians and fans preferred the blues to trad jazz, and after having dragged his feet for a while, Harold Pendleton gave Giorgio a weekly Blues Night on Thursdays at the Marquee Club. The guitarist Alexis Korner and the harmonica player Cyril Davies had put together the Blues Incorporated band to play Chicago-style electric blues, which had earthy lyrics and a great beat that appealed to teenage audiences wanting to dance. Early lineups for the

Early lineup for Blues Incorporated *(Left to Right)* Cyril Davies, Charlie Watts, Alexis Korner, Andy Hoogenboom, Keith Scott, 1962

band included Charlie Watts on drums, Dick Heckstall-Smith on saxophone, Jack Bruce on bass, and Long John Baldry on vocals.

Other young musicians would join them for a song or two, and many of them became famous, including Mick Jagger and Keith Richards, before Brian Jones started the Rolling Stones. In addition to this trio, Bill Wyman, Charlie Watts and Ian Stewart would complete the first lineup that became successful. Meanwhile, Jack Bruce and Ginger Baker became friends with Graham Bond and started the Graham Bond Organization with Dick Heckstall-Smith.

Giorgio had a chance encounter with Christine Keeler and Mandy Rice-Davies at the Blue Beat Club on Portobello

Road in Notting Hill Gate. These two models were linked to a huge political scandal involving John Profumo, a British politician who was forced to resign as the secretary of state for war in the conservative government of Harold Macmillan due to a sexual liaison with Christine Keeler. Giorgio invited the two women to come to the Marquee Club the following Thursday night. When they did, they were inevitably followed by the pack of reporters who hounded them day and night.

The following day, thanks to their visit, all the papers mentioned the Thursday night gigs at the Marquee Club, which was the best free advertising anyone could hope for. It was at the Marquee in 1962 that Giorgio also met Brian Jones. Brian and his friends were fans of Chuck Berry and Bo Diddley and emulated their style of playing the blues, which Cyril Davies disliked. Giorgio saw an opportunity to start something new in another place.

He rented the Piccadilly Club next to Piccadilly Circus on Friday nights, and invited Alexis Korner and his Blues Incorporated, the Blues by Six of Nicky Hopkins, and the Rollin' Stones (as they spelled it then) to play there, which led to a deep rift between Giorgio and Harold Pendleton, who accused Giorgio of stealing his idea and his bands.

Aware of the success of the newly-opened Ealing Club, Giorgio decided to move his venture to the suburbs too, renting the back room of the Station Hotel in Richmond in southwest London, where there was a small stage and enough room for an audience of a hundred people or so.

He produced his first concert there on January 20, 1963, and the first group he invited was the Dave Hunt Rhythm & Blues Band, with a young Ray Davies, who later became famous with the Kinks. But Giorgio fired them when they let him down one night. They were not serious enough, and he decided to replace them with the Rollin' Stones, since

Early concert by the Rolling Stones at the Crawdaddy Club c.1963

Brian Jones was constantly asking him to pay attention to his band. Giorgio called Ian Stewart, who was the only band member with a phone number, since "Stu" worked in an office at Imperial Chemical Industries, one of the largest English companies at the time.

Their first concert at the Station Hotel in Richmond on February 24, 1963, drew only three people. This could possibly be attributed to Giorgio and his misspelling of the term Rhythm and Blues, which he spelled as "Rhythm and Bulse" on the posters. The band was ready to cancel, but Giorgio encouraged them to play as if they had a full house.

Giorgio never forgot the three witnesses to this concert, which he says was absolutely phenomenal, namely Paul Williams who later had his own career as a blues singer, Little D, who became a roadie for Jimi Hendrix, and the third member of the audience, whose name he could no longer recall, became a talent agent.

Giorgio had agreed to pay a pound to each of the musicians, plus a commission per person coming in, but since there was no door to share, he gave them their promised pound and invited them to come back the following Sunday night.

From one Sunday to another, through word of mouth, more and more people came, and the band was soon playing to full capacity. Giorgio asked his assistant, Hamish Grimes, to encourage the audience to dance on the tables and gyrate their arms like windmills while the Stones played long extended versions of their Bo Diddley songs like "Pretty Thing" and "Doing the Crawdaddy" – the name which Giorgio ended up using for his club.

Each concert only lasted 45 minutes at the most, but Giorgio wanted each of these concerts to become a collective catharsis propelled by the Bo Diddley rhythm, something he told the journalists he called to promote his events, like Peter Jones of the *Record Mirror* and Patrick Doncaster of the *Daily Mirror* – one of the largest dailies in England – who came in person to the Crawdaddy and wrote a great piece on the Rollin' Stones concert he saw there.

The Stones' concerts at the Station Hotel were becoming the talk of the town, but the owner of the hotel was not happy with the commotion, and on April 22, 1963, he asked Giorgio to find another venue.

Giorgio was disappointed but his early life had given him the ability to face adversity, so he began searching for a new venue. While Giorgio was in Switzerland for his father's funeral, Hamish Grimes asked Harold Pendleton to recommend him to Commander Wheeler who ran the Richmond Athletic Association, where the National Jazz and Blues Festival was held and which was located not too far from the Station Hotel.

Giorgio moved the Crawdaddy Club there, and with a much larger space, he could now welcome up to a thousand people for more important concerts. The Rolling Stones played there, as well as the Paramounts (future Procol

Harum), the Moody Blues, the Muleskinners (before Ian McLagan joined the Small Faces), the Animals, and Steampacket with Rod Stewart.

On August 10 and 11 of 1963, Giorgio organized the third annual National Jazz and Blues Festival at the Richmond Athletic Grounds, where he managed to book the Rolling Stones and Long John Baldry *(see below)*.

One year later, thanks to the opening that Giorgio had managed to make in the 1963 program, the fourth Annual Jazz and Blues Festival included the Rolling Stones and the T-Bones on Friday, August 7; the Long John Baldry Hoochie Coochie Men and Manfred Mann on August 8; and the Graham Bond Organization, Georgie Fame and the Blue Flames, and the Yardbirds on the evening of August 9.

Famous bluesmen were also on the bill, such as Mose Allison, Jimmy Witherspoon, and Memphis Slim, as well as Chris Barber and several other jazz bands from the London area. During these years of 1963 and 1964, Giorgio's influence on the scene was undeniable, and he managed to

The Rolling Stones play the National Jazz and Blues Festival
at the Richmond Athletic Ground in 1963

find investment to set up his own label, Marmalade Records.

In spite of all of this, the Rolling Stones never played the Crawdaddy Club after their concert of September 22, 1963 as their single "Come on" recorded on May 10th, 1963 had propelled the group to stardom and playing at bigger venues.

Giorgio organized a concert by the Yardbirds at the Club A'Gogo in Newcastle on December 13, 1963. The Animals were there, and he invited them to play at his Crawdaddy Club in order to get the attention of the London crowd.

To celebrate his 30th birthday on February 28, 1964, Giorgio organized an important concert. This was indeed the first chapter of the Rhythm & Blues Festival in Birmingham, with the Yardbirds, the Spencer Davis Group (featuring a 15-year-old Stevie Winwood, who sang and played the organ), the Roadrunners (a band from Liverpool), Sonny Boy Williamson, Rod Stewart, and Long John Baldry's Hoochie Coochie Men.

Giorgio had an innate talent for collaboration which helped him build a team of people who would work with him for years. The two main members of his team were Enid Tidey, who had already proved herself with Denis Preston, the first independent music producer to have his own recording studio and his own record label in England,

 and the photographer Hamish Grimes, whose introduction of the band can be heard at the start of the album *Five Live Yardbirds*, which was recorded in front of an audience at the Marquee on March 20, 1964.

"Brian and I ... I kind of let myself be a friend of his because we were both born on the 28th of February. You can't go wrong, born on the same day. It's not the same year, but the same day. Pisces, lunatics. Big mistake...
I warned him. I told him, I have no doubt that you'll get there, but be careful when you get there. I warned him. I was four or five years older than him. Not that much, you know." – GOMELSKY

Giorgio Gomelsky as MC *(Left)* Brian Jones, 1965 *(Above)*
(Bottom) Back room of the pub where the Crawdaddy Club was located in Richmond, Surrey.

The Rolling Stones in the early 1960s. Photo: Mike Peters

The Beatles in the early 1960s

4.THE STONES & THE BEATLES

The Rolling Stones

By organizing early gigs for the band, and seeking publicity, Giorgio became their 'de facto' manager without ever signing a contract. Brian Jones and Ian Stewart were the two founders and organizers of the band, but Brian was the leader. Brian envied the budding fame of the Beatles and dreamed of becoming famous, something he would harp on about when they were unloading the equipment or sticking promo posters up on lamp posts for their concerts.

Due to some publicity which Giorgio managed to get for the band, the Stones were suddenly in the public eye and Giorgio got them into a small recording studio to cut two songs that they often played on stage – one by Jimmy Reed (most probably "Honest I Do") and one by Bo Diddley (most probably "You Can't Judge a Book By Looking at the Cover") – but these recordings have long disappeared and were never heard by anybody outside Giorgio's close circle.

Then Giorgio decided to shoot a promo film for these "illustrious unknowns," which was a kind of early form of music video and innovative at the time. He brought them to the RG Jones Studio in Wimbledon, where two songs were filmed with extra scenes for cutaways. While he was working on the film editing, he received a call from a journalist who asked him for the name of the club where the Rolling Stones were playing for an article he was about to write. Giorgio had to think on his feet and he knew that BR&B – or British Rhythm and Blues – was not ideal, and then the Bo Diddley song that the Stones used to end their concerts, "Doing the Crawdaddy," came to mind and he replied, "The Crawdaddy."

When he got back to London from his father's funeral in Switzerland, he wanted to show the band how much work he had done with their promo film. Brian Jones came to the studio with his "friend" Andrew Loog Oldham, and that's how Giorgio found out that Brian had just signed a management contract with Andrew, a young public school educated Englishman who had worked for Brian Epstein and the Beatles.

Giorgio was a few years older than the Stones, but Andrew was the same age as the band, and may have been more on their wavelength. Perhaps more importantly, Andrew was quintessentially English, and Giorgio was an outsider with his thick European accent. Whenever he spoke about it, Giorgio always mentioned English xenophobia with disdain.

"Brian sold out for a ten guinea suit."– GOMELSKY

Brian Jones, circa 1963. Photo: Mike Peters

Giorgio was deeply hurt. He had believed that Brian was a close and true friend, and that both of them were working together with the same goal and ideals for the band.

He never forgave Brian for this betrayal, and it weighed heavily on him for years. When Giorgio spoke of Brian later, he would imitate his lisp, despite the fact that Brian had an unfortunate early death.

Both Bill Wyman in his *Stone Alone* book, and Keith Richards in his biography, *Life*, would acknowledge Giorgio's contribution and the shameful way that he was booted from the band, especially after all the effort he had put into promoting them.

The Beatles

In the summer of 1961, Giorgio met the Beatles in Hamburg while he was touring with Chris Barber, and he met them again with their manager Brian Epstein during their first trips to London.

The Beatles in Hamburg. Early lineup with Stuart Sutcliffe, 1961

Filmmaking was Giorgio's first vocation, and he had actually started making a film with the Rolling Stones that few people have seen and which has since disappeared. Giorgio maintained that Mick Jagger was probably responsible for this eventuality.

Giorgio then suggested to Brian Epstein that he could make a film with the Beatles, a kind of documentary of one day in the crazy life of the band, but according to Giorgio, Brian Epstein understood little about the artistic potential of movies, and he turned the idea down.

When the film *A Hard Day's Night* was released a year and a half later, Giorgio was extremely frustrated. He couldn't believe that Brian Epstein had stolen his idea and given it to the filmmakers without telling him anything about it or giving him any credit. Their business relationship was impacted as Giorgio was naturally very angry with Brian Epstein at the time.

Whether Epstein felt guilty or not, he did go some way to making things right by letting the Yardbirds open for the Beatles at their Christmas shows two years in a row, and the Yardbirds were the support act for the Beatles on their European tour in the spring of 1965.

It was Giorgio who introduced the Beatles to the Rolling Stones when the Liverpool four came to Richmond to see the Stones play at the Crawdaddy Club in April 1963. A kind of friendly rivalry grew up between the two bands that lasted for many years.

THE STONES & THE BEATLES

"The Beatles took every f***ing chance that they could ...
McCartney was the one you could talk to about anything.
Lennon not so much. Lennon was a skeptic."

"The Beatles came to my club and they saw the Rolling
Stones, the Illustrious Unknowns. It was at the Station
Hotel... and then we went back to the Stones' house
and we listened to music all night long."

"George Martin would not have known what to do with
the Stones... The blues aspect. George Martin was not
into the blues." – GOMELSKY

"At the Station Hotel, we were so packed, that the boys who were bringing girls had to bring the girls on their shoulders. There was no room on the floor... We were the first club to ask the audience to participate – in the second set in particular."
– GOMELSKY

The Yardbirds c. 1966, *(Left to right)* guitarist Jeff Beck, drummer Jim McCarty, rhythm guitarist Chris Dreja, guitarist Jimmy Page and singer Keith Relf

5. THE YARDBIRDS

Having lost the Rolling Stones, Giorgio had to replace them for his weekly concerts at the Crawdaddy. He found a new band, the Yardbirds, who started fairly quickly after the departure of the Stones. But this time, he armed himself with a management contract for his own protection, and he also established himself as their record producer.

It was Hamish Grimes who took Giorgio to see a band rehearsing in a room above a pub in East Sheen, near Richmond and, as he walked up the stairs, Giorgio was instantly seduced by the wild beat that he could hear coming from the room. He opened the door, waited for the end of the song, and the first thing he told them was, "You're hired!"

The Yardbirds took their name from an expression used by Jack Kerouac to describe migrant workers who travelled for free by jumping from one train to another in freight cars. The members of the band were: Keith Relf on vocals and blues harp, Paul-Samwell Smith on bass guitar, Chris Dreja on rhythm guitar, Jim McCarty on drums, and Anthony "Top" Topham on lead guitar.

However, Top Topham was only 15 years old and was not allowed by his parents to go on tour with the band as he was still at school. Giorgio knew that he would have to be replaced sooner rather than later. He recruited Eric Clapton, an 18-year-old friend of Top Topham, who joined the band in October 1963. Under the musical leadership of Paul Samwell-Smith, the Yardbirds' style was based on a blend of blues and rock, featuring improvisations that slowed down only to speed up again in an orgasmic manner, according to the beat.

Thanks to this new approach, which Giorgio called the "rave up," the Yardbirds quickly became *the* group to see live on stage, but their first studio recordings were not successful. In 1964, Giorgio signed a recording contract for the band with Columbia for England and Epic for the United States, but their first single, "I Wish You Would," was a flop. Their second single, "Good Morning Little School Girl," hardly made an impression and reached only number 44 on the hit parade.

Giorgio worked closely with the innovative technicians of the time including Jim Marshall, the man behind the famous Marshall guitar amplifiers, and Tom Jennings, of the Vox amplifiers, who both helped him get a better sound on his live recordings in a way that was unmatched during 1963 and 1964.

The sound engineer Keith Grant, who would later record all the English rock nobility of the 1960s at Olympic Studios, brought one of his reel-to-reel tape recorders from his studio to the Crawdaddy for the concert of Sonny Boy Williamson and the Yardbirds on December 8, 1963. Giorgio was very happy with the quality of the recording, which was remarkable indeed for a 1963 live recording, but the record was only released two years later on January 7, 1966. Later on, copies of copies were made and sold with an obvious loss of audio quality, which disappointed the buyers who were unaware of the duplication.

Sonny Boy Williamson had come to Europe in October of 1963 with the second annual tour of the American Folk Blues Festival, where Giorgio met him, as he was handling

Sonny Boy Williamson with harmonica

the English leg of the tour. When Sonny Boy decided to stay in Europe, Giorgio let him stay at his place when he came to London. Giorgio told me that he used to leave one of the windows half open at the back of the house so that Sonny Boy could let himself in and sleep on the living room sofa.

It is well known that Sonny Boy's temper could be pretty bad, and he did not make it easy on the English musicians who were backing him. A striking example of his temper was immortalized by Leonard Chess, who kept the acerbic exchange recorded in the studio between Leonard and Sonny Boy, as an intro to the song "Little Village". This inspired John Hyatt, Nick Lowe, Ry Cooder, and Jim Keltner to name their band "Little Village" in 1981.

Eric Clapton during his time with the Yardbirds c.1964

Back in the States after his tour in England, Sonny Boy made this rather caustic statement: "Those British boys want to play the blues really bad – and they do!"

This was around the time that Giorgio nicknamed Eric Clapton "Slowhand," because it always took him ages to change a broken guitar string while the audience waited and slowly clapped.

The Yardbirds lived through three separate and distinct eras with three remarkable guitar players – Eric Clapton, Jeff Beck, and Jimmy Page. Each one eventually developed his own original style and became a "guitar hero," but their personal relationships with Giorgio were not always congenial. Most of the band had been friends since their student days at Kingston Art School. They knew each other well and had started a band called the Metropolitan Blues Quartet in 1962. Clapton had dropped out of Kingston Art School after a year and formed a duo with Dave Brock (who later co founded Hawkwind) to play in pubs around the area.

Unusually, Eric had been brought up by his maternal grandparents, thinking that his mother was his older sister. His mother was only 16 years old when he was born, and his father was a Canadian soldier who had returned to Canada. A few years later, his mother moved to Canada with another Canadian soldier. Eric was 9 years old when he was told the truth and found out that his older sister was really his mother. The mental shock was huge and would haunt him for years.

He was a shy loner, and during the various trips with the other members of the band, he sat in a corner of the van and kept to himself. He had a tendency to be a bit aggressive and could be easily provoked by the others. When they had long hair, he cut his in a crew cut, and when the others cut theirs shorter, he grew his longer.

He did not get along with Paul Samwell-Smith, who was the musical director of the band, but on the positive side, he was able to channel his negative energy ferociously into his guitar solos.

When Giorgio and Hamish Grimes had to replace Eric Clapton following his decision to leave the band, they paid a visit to Jeff Beck, on the recommendation of Jimmy Page, to see him play with his band, the Tridents. They were quickly convinced that Jeff would be perfect and so invited him to audition (Giorgio recalled that the audition was held at the Marquee in February 1965, others like Top Topham remembered that it was held at The Railway Tavern opposite the Station Hotel.)

Although his scruffy look and black leather jacket were not to the taste of the others, when Jeff plugged his guitar into an amp and began to play, he soon persuaded them otherwise.

Now that Eric was out and Jeff was in, Giorgio inherited another loner who didn't talk much. But while Eric took great care of his physical appearance, Jeff's hair was often dirty, and his jeans were sometimes oil-stained as he loved to tinker with the engines of sports cars in his spare time. His black leather jacket only added to the impression of him being a hoodlum.

Moreover, his health was weak, and he didn't enjoy long trips, particularly when Giorgio used to drive the band around in a van to save money. Jeff's health problems came on top of Keith Relf's – Keith was asthmatic, had a tendency to drink too much, and often passed out – which made Giorgio feel like he was babysitting a bunch of children in diapers.

It was on stage that Jeff expressed himself emotionally through his guitar playing, and he would be intensely irritated if he had technical problems with his amplifiers, to the point of smashing them up.

The Yardbirds in 1965. *(Left to right, top to bottom)* Jeff Beck, Paul Samwell-Smith, Keith Relf, Chris Dreja and Jim McCarty
Photo: Beat Publications

Giorgio recalled that during their first American tour, the Yardbirds' equipment had not arrived in time, so he had asked Chuck Berry to lend him an amplifier for Jeff but, perhaps wisely, Chuck only agreed to sell him one. Finally, Giorgio succeeded in borrowing a small Fender amp from the Beach Boys, which Jeff managed to break.

When Paul Samwell-Smith decided to stop playing bass to focus on the production and engineering aspect of recordings, Chris Dreja picked up the bass guitar, and Jeff became the only guitar player on stage, playing both rhythm and lead guitars.

Giorgio had previously asked Jimmy Page to replace Eric Clapton, but Jimmy had refused, as he didn't want to upset Eric and run the risk of ruining their friendship. Jimmy was extremely talented and well-known for the session work he had done with many bands, including the Kinks, the Who, and Them. His excellent studio experience had also taught him the art of music production and the reading of arrangements and musical scores.

By then, Jimmy was tired of working for others, and he wanted to find musicians to collaborate with. When the opportunity came his way again to join the Yardbirds, he jumped at the chance. It was no longer a case of replacing somebody, but rather of filling a gap.

Jimmy had a more sociable personality, and he told them that he would be happy to play any instrument they wanted, even the bass or the tambourine. He actually did start on bass before switching to the guitar, on which he traded licks with his friend Jeff.

Unfortunately, this did not last long, because even though Jeff seemed to enjoy having his friend Jimmy in the band at first, he soon grew tired of it all and announced his departure from the band on November 30, 1966, while they were on a disastrous American tour, travelling in the uncomfortable buses of Dick Clark's Caravan of the Stars. Jeff suddenly left the tour and went to see his friend Mary Hughes in San Francisco. Since Peter Grant was about to take over as the band's manager, Giorgio didn't have to resolve this problem.

Giorgio fully managed the first and second legs of the Yardbirds' career, and the period with Jeff Beck was undoubtedly the most creative and the most popular time.

Eric Clapton left the Yardbirds just as they had their first big success with "For Your Love," a song written by Graham Gouldman, whom Giorgio got to know well and who would pen two more hits for the band: "Evil Hearted You" and "Heart Full of Soul".

As soon as Giorgio heard the intro of "For Your Love," he knew that this was the song the band needed to break the musical mold they were stuck in, and that just like the Beatles, the Rolling Stones, the Kinks, and the Who, the time had come for them to move away from pure rhythm'n' blues towards a more lucrative popular market.

However, by taking the band in more of a pop direction, this caused Eric Clapton to quit the band, and he went on to join John Mayall and his Bluesbreakers, and later on to start Cream with Jack Bruce and Ginger Baker, two alumni of Alexis Korner's Blues Incorporated who had played with the Graham Bond Organization, and also briefly with John Mayall before partnering with Clapton.

Giorgio vividly remembered the day that he spent in his Soho Square office in January 1965, from two in the afternoon till ten at night, trying to persuade Eric to stay with the Yardbirds. But Eric's mind was made up. He wanted to play the blues, pure and simple, whereas Giorgio was looking for a more commercial offering for the band.

It may have been that the famous graffiti on a wall in London – "Clapton Is God" – had gone to his head, but Giorgio believed that it was more a matter of Eric being ill-at-ease with the band's 'rave up' style and their exploration of different musical territories. Giorgio tried to encourage Eric to go further down the road of experimentation and was telling him not to be afraid, because the music was becoming really exceptional, but he could see that Eric wasn't really comfortable artistically.

When Jeff Beck came onto the scene, he immediately gave a creative impetus to the band, and their music started to move away from the pure form of blues that Eric had mastered. Jeff immersed himself fully in the pursuit of new sounds, which were then a challenge to reproduce on stage.

As a producer, Giorgio also brought his own brand of creativity. He even sang on "A Certain Girl" and found the Indian musician who brought his sitar for "Heart Full of Soul" – even if the sitar part was eventually replaced by Jeff, who managed to produce a similar sound on his guitar.

It was also Giorgio who suggested that they record the first and probably only Gregorian chant to become a hit in the English charts, "Still I'm Sad," in which he sang the bass part and played the triangle. The genesis of this song, which was probably one of the first to be written by the band, was actually quite interesting.

It was when Giorgio and the band went to the bathroom before a concert at Aylesbury Town Hall, that he happened to start humming something in that style. The echo in the bathroom was excellent, so Keith joined him, then Paul Samwell-Smith joined in and the three of them were surprised to hear that something special was happening.

Paul then wrote the song, and the group went to a studio to record the instrumental part and gathered around a mike with Giorgio on August 17, 1965. What had started as a bit of larking about in a bathroom helped the song become a highly distinctive hit record. Giorgio also sang the bass part with them when they later performed the song on stage.

In the USA, Giorgio took on the van driving to save money on their first tour which was especially difficult as Giorgio had not really understood the distances involved or the unreliability of the venues. Jeff Beck would later complain of the trials and tribulations he had to endure at the hands of the "Mad Russian" during that month of September 1965.

Giorgio had long wondered how American producers like Phil Spector in Los Angeles, Sam Phillips in Memphis, and the brothers Leonard and Phil Chess in Chicago, had managed to produce such an authentic sound of the drums, particularly the bass drum, something which he complained that the English sound engineers were unable to duplicate.

After an incident with local rednecks in Little Rock, Arkansas, they drove all night and arrived in Memphis at six in the morning, on September 12, 1965, intending to lay down two tracks at Sun Records. But it was Sunday, and Sam Phillips, the legendary producer who gave life to the careers of Elvis Presley, Carl Perkins, Johnny Cash, Jerry Lee Lewis, Roy Orbison, and many others, wasn't there, as he had apparently gone fishing. Giorgio and the band waited patiently for Sam to return, and when he finally came in around midnight with his fishing rod in hand, he was in no mood to start working, having had a few drinks, which did not help much either.

Giorgio took a roll of greenbacks out of his pocket and offered him 600 dollars. Sam took it, and drank a couple of cups of coffee, Giorgio stepped in as his sound assistant, everything fell into place, and the recording session finally ended at 7 a.m. They had worked all night to record "You're a Better Man Than I" and "The Train Kept a-Rollin'," both of which became long-term successes for them.

Although the session had started with a reluctant Sam Phillips at the helm, it ended in harmony at 10 a.m. with breakfast and Wild Turkey in Sam's hotel suite at the local Holiday Inn.

Three months later, on December 21, at Chess Records in Chicago, Giorgio repeated the process. They recorded the hits "I'm a Man" and, more importantly, "Shapes of Things," an original track with a pacifist message that chimed with the feelings of the new protest movement of young people who opposed the Vietnam War and who refused to become cannon fodder for the American army fighting in Southeast Asia.

"Shapes of Things" was the product of one of the long drives across America at night. Dave Brubeck's music was on the radio and Giorgio suggested to Paul Samwell-Smith that a riff like that would make an excellent bass line.

At 2 a.m., in the bar of the Holiday Inn where they were staying, they wrote a song based on a similar riff, which they recorded a few hours later. Jeff Beck's solo was recorded twice, and Giorgio used one part of one take and another part of the other take for the final mix. The whole thing was produced in mono as was usual at the time.

It was the track "The Train Kept a-Rollin'" that best illustrated Giorgio's musical originality and ability to tune into the zeitgeist – something he understood perfectly well, since it was the subtitle he chose when Charly Records later released the 4 CD Yardbirds boxset: *Train Kept a-Rollin': The Complete Giorgio Gomelsky Recordings* in 1993.

My friend Larry Birnbaum, the writer of many articles on world music, and husband of one of my wife Lilian's best friends, was an expert on the origins of the blues and on the influence it has had on different styles of music that came after it in America and the rest of the world. Larry and Giorgio were also friends, and Giorgio invited him often to his private parties. Larry and I spent hours talking about music. His expertise was more about the different forms of American blues, while mine was more about English covers, such as the many tracks by Muddy Waters which were covered by the Rolling Stones, both in official and bootleg releases.

On November 22, 1992, Larry was visiting us at home and he explained the origin of "The Train Kept a-Rollin'" which goes back to "Cow-Cow Boogie," a hit for the Freddie Slack Orchestra with vocalist Ella Mae Morse in 1942, at a time when boogie-woogie music was made popular by the big bands of Glenn Miller, Tommy Dorsey, and the Andrews Sisters. One of the most prolific composers of the genre was Don Raye, whose title "Down the Road Apiece" was covered by Amos Wilburn, Chuck Berry, the Rolling Stones, and others. His title "The House of Blue Lights" was covered by Chuck Berry, Canned Heat, George Thorogood, and many more.

On October 6, 1951, in Cincinnati, Tiny Bradshaw recorded "The Train Kept a-Rollin'," which he authored and which became the model for the song we know today, even if the rhythm is in a jump-blues style. Then, on July 2, 1956, in Nashville, Johnny Burnette recorded the first rockabilly version, with an electric guitar riff that would later be used by Jeff Beck and the Yardbirds.

When a song goes through so many transformations, the lyrics tend to be modified, and in this case, it even happened to the title, which went from "Cow-Cow Boogie" to "The Train Kept a-Rollin'," where the chorus, "The train kept a-rollin' / All night long!" was repeated in a call and response style between the main singer

Larry Birnbaum in 1992

and the backup singers, an exchange that the audience could easily remember.

From a purely musical point of view, two common sounds that people heard daily in the country and on the plantations were the sounds of the passing trains and the cackling of the hens. Many guitarists have reproduced these sounds on their electric guitars, and Jeff Beck was working on the whistle of the train sound when the idea to record a cover of "The Train Kept a-Rollin'" took shape – a song that Jeff had already played with Screaming Lord Sutch during his brief stay with him in 1964.

Moreover, besides a new, radical instrumental treatment, Keith Relf sang two versions of the lyrics that were not exactly identical but that Giorgio decided to keep although they overlapped each other here and there. Giorgio recorded additional parts on September 21 and 22, 1965, with Roy Halee, the sound engineer of Columbia Recording Studios in New York, before mixing the two vocal tracks of Keith Relf right there and then.

Roy Halee was the sound engineer who, after his work with the Yardbirds, the Lovin' Spoonful, and the Dave Clark Five, produced the recordings of Simon and Garfunkel, both together and in their solo careers, and his work was recognized with Grammys for "Mrs. Robinson" and "Bridge over Troubled Water." He also worked with the Byrds, Journey, Blood Sweat and Tears, Laura Nyro, and many others.

It's also worth mentioning that these recordings of the Yardbirds in the studios of Sun Records and Columbia were made in secret during the night, since the band had neither the visas nor the record company contracts to make any of their recordings in the U.S.

"The Train Kept a-Rollin'" was not released as a single by the Yardbirds in England, but this song became one of their most popular numbers. At first, they included it in practically all their concerts until their breakup in the spring of 1968. But the influence it has had on several generations of musicians, such as Aerosmith, Foghat, Twisted Sister, Hanoi Rocks, Stray Cats, and many others, continues today.

Jimmy Page continued to play it with the New Yardbirds, as we can hear in the album *Farewell Concert* recorded on March 30, 1968, at the Anderson Theater in New York – and even with Led Zeppelin, as we can hear in the recording of their concert of June 20, 1980, in Brussels.

Giorgio was right to be proud of having produced this track, but all the recordings of the Yardbirds that he had produced up to that point had only really been singles. Giorgio was aware of this when he released the LP *Five Live Yardbirds* – the live recording of their concert at the Marquee Club on March 20, 1964 with Eric Clapton – so that he could release an album where the style of all the songs had real homogeneity, even if the tape had to be slightly sped up so that all the songs could fit on the two sides of the record.

As Giorgio also explained, pop fans of the time mainly bought singles, whereas blues aficionados bought mostly LPs. *Five Live Yardbirds* gave him the chance to reach out to an audience of blues fans too.

Five Live Yardbirds was also one of the first LPs that were recorded live and released by a rock band. The crew arrived at the Marquee at 1 p.m. to set up the equipment, the Yardbirds played two 45-minute concerts in late afternoon and in the evening, everything was recorded in one day, and

the best versions of each song were selected later on.

The aim was to capture the atmosphere of the club. Actually, Giorgio used a similar technique in the studio, where he first recorded all the musicians of the rhythm section together until he had one take that reflected the true feeling and sound of the live band, then he recorded the vocals and solos separately – all in superb mono.

Giorgio told me several times how fundamental this was. He didn't like musicians who used dozens of layers and audio effects, nor did he like those who made recordings at home by mixing together several digital tracks, without ever being able to create the sound of a real band. He also preferred guitar players who could create their vibrato sounds by pushing the strings with their fingers on the neck of their guitar, rather than those who used a tremolo arm. In most cases, Giorgio believed that the new technologies contributed little to creativity, and that they did not motivate musicians to actually play together and produce a contagious rhythm for a live audience.

The other Yardbirds LPs produced by Giorgio were just compilations of singles that lacked homogeneity of style and sound, but that had to be released to satisfy the record companies in the UK and in the USA as they needed to have new products on the shelves of the record stores. As a producer, his successful output of hits during 1965 and 1966 was undeniable, but he also made commercial choices that were at odds with the band.

One example of this is when Giorgio booked the Yardbirds to play at the San Remo Festival in Italy in January 1966, in front of an audience that was more used to pop singers. It is possible that Giorgio wanted to find a new audience and open new doors, but the musicians had a different ambition – they wanted to be on a par with their contemporaries such as the Beatles, the Rolling Stones, the

Who, the Kinks, etc.

Moreover, Giorgio had them record two Italian songs: "Paff...Bum" (which they sang in English) and the pop ballad "Questa Volta" (Jeff Beck did not even play on this one) to try and please the local audience, but neither number proved popular. The idea was not original, since Brian Epstein had done the same with the Beatles releasing German versions of "I Want to Hold Your Hand," which became "Komm, Gib Mir Deine Hand," and "She Loves You," which became "Sie Liebt Dich." Both were released on a single in Germany on March 5, 1964.

Two months after the Yardbirds' tried to make inroads into the Italian pop scene, the Rolling Stones had a go at it with their version of "As Tears Go By," which became in Italian "Con Le Mie Lacrime" and which they recorded on March 15, 1966, to be released as a single with "Heart of Stone." This record did not fare much better either.

In trying to capture the European market, the Beatles and the Rolling Stones had released songs that had already been successful in English. But "Questa Volta" was not even

The Yardbirds in San Remo with pop singer Bobby Solo, 1966

a Yardbirds' composition, and "Paff… Bum," originally written for Italian singer Lucio Dalla by Gian Franco Reverberi, with Italian lyrics by Sergio Bardotti, was given English lyrics by Paul Samwell-Smith.

Giorgio also had ideas to develop the sound of the band in new directions. He suggested the addition of a keyboard player, as synthesizers were becoming popular at the time, and he thought that Keith Emerson, a musician from Brighton, might be a contender.

Thanks to his father, Giorgio was given an exceptional and eclectic music education that included Arab and African music, Stockhausen, and Xenakis. As his mother was a hat designer and aware of changing trends in fashion, Giorgio was also able to recognise new cultural trends and ideas, particularly in music. It was Giorgio who pushed the Yardbirds to use feedback as a sound effect, something which Eric Clapton happened to get one day when he left his guitar against his amplifier on his way to the bathroom. Giorgio thought of using a harpsichord on "For Your Love," and he introduced a sitar player for "Heart Full of Soul." His regular lunches with the sound engineers allowed

him to keep abreast of any new sound effects they had come up with – sometimes by chance – that he could use in his new recordings.

The bass player and musical director, Paul Samwell-Smith, was increasingly unhappy with playing gigs, due to the challenges of dealing with Keith Relf and his worsening drinking problem, and an irascible Jeff Beck. He decided

Paul Samwell-Smith, c.1965

to focus entirely on the production and composition side of their recordings. The famous nameless album, which everyone knows as Roger the Engineer, was released with a production credit for Paul and his friend Simon Napier-Bell, and this was the end of the road for Giorgio as a producer for the Yardbirds.

Although he retained the rights to the recordings that he had produced with them, the original tapes were, perhaps inevitably, used by others and reissued in various compilations. Unfortunately, Giorgio did not receive any royalties from these reissues while other producers had the benefit of the sales revenue.

These changes at the heart of the musical organization of the band became even more dramatic when Jeff Beck decided to leave and Jimmy Page took over. Then the new manager Simon Napier-Bell suggested that Giorgio should be replaced by Peter Grant, another force of nature.

The endless tours had been exhausting and not really profitable, and the band members themselves were still broke. In spite of Giorgio's efforts, neither he nor the individual members of the Yardbirds were able to enjoy long-term benefits from their success. The time had come to move in a more lucrative direction.

Giorgio never managed to gain the same success in the eyes of the public again, although his name would forever be associated with the Yardbirds. This huge but fleeting success would forever stick to him despite his best efforts to reinvent himself in other ways.

Steampacket. (*Left to right*) Rod Stewart, Long John Baldry, Julie Driscoll and Brian Auger, 1965. Photo: Dezo Hoffman

6. PARAGON PUBLICITY AND MARMALADE RECORDS

"Most bands did not have a clue as to what to do in the studio... Everybody can sound beautiful on their instruments, but when you put them together, they sound like shit. How many people can you put in a phone booth?" – GOMELSKY

Giorgio opened his public relations company, Paragon Publicity, in 1965 and Marmalade Records in 1966. He also worked as a sound engineer for the recording of the French rock star Johnny Hallyday's LP *La Génération Perdue (The Lost Generation)*, which was recorded at the Olympic Sound Studio in London, and released on October 17, 1966.

In 1967, Giorgio obtained financing from Polydor, the German record label that distributed his records, and he was suddenly "rolling in the dough." His office was the meeting place of the Swingin' London scene, with musicians such as the Rolling Stones, the Beatles, and the Yardbirds dropping in, as well as artists of all kinds, producers, directors, and, of course, lots of attractive, young women.

During the day, the office was like a creative beehive, with eight full-time employees. At night, parties were in full swing until the cleaning ladies came in at the break of dawn.

Paragon and Marmalade took care of new artists like John McLaughlin, Julie Driscoll, Brian Auger and the

Trinity, Blossom Toes, Graham Gouldman, and Savage Rose (a prog-rock band from Denmark), and Giorgio also produced demos for Jeff Beck, Jimmy Page, Alexis Korner, Graham Bond, Soft Machine, and Rod Stewart. But his two most important musical productions for Marmalade were "This Wheel's on Fire," and *Extrapolation.*

"This Wheel's on Fire," a Bob Dylan song sung by Julie Driscoll with Brian Auger and the Trinity, climbed to fifth place on the English hit parade in June of 1968. It was a true example of psychedelic music, with its distortion effects and the heavy sound of the organ and the mellotron.

Extrapolation, the first LP of John McLaughlin, was recorded on January 18, 1969, at Advision Studio. One year later, McLaughlin recorded with Miles Davis, and he found fame with a wider audience thanks to the recording of his Mahavishnu Orchestra in 1971.

Marmalade's recording studio was also used as a rehearsal studio for touring bands like the Doors and Otis Redding.

For fun, Giorgio put together Monday comedy nights at the Speakeasy with the likes of Brian Auger, Eric Burdon, Jimi Hendrix, and Keith Moon in a style that was reprised by Monthy Python a few months later on the BBC.

Giorgio continued to work with the many musicians he had known at the Crawdaddy, such as Long John Baldry, or struggling artists like the very young Rod Stewart.

However, after two productive and heavenly years, Polydor closed the cash register and, reluctantly, Giorgio was forced to close his offices. Not only that, but Giorgio had fathered another child, a daughter called Alexandra. His relationship with Alexandra's mother soon fell apart and in 1969, he left London, never to return, and moved to Paris.

***

Marmalade offices, June 8, 1967. (*Left to right*) Madeleine Hirsiger, an office colleague, Julie Driscoll, and Giorgio Gomelsky. Photo courtesy of Madeleine Carr.

Madeleine Carr (born Hirsiger), was born in England in 1943, raised in Switzerland, and moved to London in October 1964, where she met Giorgio before returning to Geneva in 1965. After two months, Giorgio met her there to drive her to Paris and see the Yardbirds' concert at the Palais des Sports, where they were opening for the Beatles on June 20, 1965.

She worked at the offices of Paragon Publicity and Marmalade Records from 1965 to 1969, and her contribution below describes what it was like working there.

She met Giorgio again in New York in 1984 when she was in transit between Berlin and Tallahassee. At other times, Giorgio met up with her in Macon, Georgia, and in Florida.

While they were in Florida, large groups of butterflies were flying around them; Giorgio ducked to avoid them and said, "Butterflies everywhere... They don't bite, do they?" Later she wrote in an email: "I always thought that it symbolized how our lives split in 1969."

***

This is how Madeleine remembers her life at Giorgio Gomelsky's Paragon and Marmalade's London offices from 1965 to 1969 in a message she sent me from Florida on August 14, 2017:

"In June 1965 the crowds of people along Lac Léman, Geneva, were just gathering when I decided to go back to my rented room to change for the evening. Madame reluctantly announced I had had a telephone call and he would call back momentarily.

I had landed in Geneva in May that year, running away from an 8-month gig at the National Jazz Federation on Wardour Street in London. I was 21, young, confused, and wondering how I could honestly help the crew I saw gathered at the corner office on the first floor above the coffee shop.

The telephone call came. Giorgio Gomelsky had rediscovered my whereabouts and wondered whether I wanted to go to Paris with him. He was just passing through on his way from Italy in his Lancia. He needed to get to Paris for a June concert at the Palais des Sports. The Yardbirds were the opening act for the Beatles. And of course, it being a Saturday afternoon and me not expected back until Monday morning, I agreed.

Giorgio promised a plane ticket back from Paris to Geneva. His favorite car was a Lancia, and at some point before we reached Paris the day before the concert, I drove, and we stopped in an open area and slept in the car.

In Paris, walking down the Champs Élysées, the Beatles (eating lobster at an outdoor restaurant) greeted us, and we

74

went to a small hotel. I shared the room with Giorgio (two beds), we drove with the Yardbirds to the venue, and that was my memory from that weekend.

Giorgio had called me because he wanted to persuade me to return to London to work with him as his assistant. He (and his partner Enid) had moved from the Wardour Street office to Ladbroke Grove, where he also maintained his office for a year or so. Working for Gomelsky Associates, I met the Rolling Stones and many others who came into that office. We were planning a unique concert with Manfred Mann that was scripted, etc.

At Ladbroke Grove, in addition to Enid there was another acquaintance called Militza, supposedly a Romanian princess. Since Giorgio's father was from Georgia, and Giorgio had lived in Ticino, Switzerland, it would not surprise me that he met her through one of the expats living there.

One reason I met Giorgio was that I, too, was Swiss, and had organized jazz festivals in Zurich with André Berner. My connection grew from that to Harold Pendleton, head of the National Jazz Federation in London, where I was offered a job (I was involved with Pendleton and the third Richmond Jazz Festival as well in 1963). Imagine my surprise when I was told I was to work with Giorgio, whom I knew by reputation from the Lugano Jazz Festival. We got along fine. I learned very early on to interpret his eccentric views and put them into action.

When I opened the office door at Wardour Street in 1965 (I arrived in October that year), I was taken aback at the long-haired guys sitting on the desk. That was new to me – the hair, and the music as well. It was Keith Relf and the other members of the Yardbirds. I had hoped for more in-depth connections with the jazz scene, so this really threw me.

Before I "escaped" back to Switzerland, I realized that my job was to keep the groups and their road managers in check. I made appointments with tailors to have suits fitted, I woke musicians up in the mornings, I arranged interviews. It was all a bit too far out for me. Giorgio arrived one day with Eric Clapton's replacement that he'd met at the barbershop on Wardour Street (that street was also the home of the Marquee Club).

Sonny Boy Williamson and many others were in the office, and one day, in the apartment I was sharing with Dixieland musician Chris Barber's sister Audrey Barber in Shepherd's Bush, we had a party with Big Mama Thornton, some of the Yardbirds, the Rolling Stones, and others I do not remember. It was a very loud and musically beautiful gathering for an impromptu jam session. Giorgio, of course, was there as well.

Anyway, I agreed to return to London in the summer of 1965. One reason was that Giorgio convinced me that, with the backing of Polydor Records, he was going to start a company that would incorporate management, booking, design, and public relations. It was to be called Paragon Publicity and Public Relations, Ltd. The offices were adjacent to Polydor on Stratford Place off Oxford Street.

And what offices. Giorgio's was at the end of a long corridor. The door had a mirror that reflected the Michael Grimes-designed psychedelic hall, outfitted with arches in orange, purple, yellow, and red with a hand-sewn carpet. His office was almost black. An elaborate custom-made wrought iron base and glass top desk almost filled the entire room. His office opened onto mine through double doors, on both sides of which were evocative art nouveau designs.

The management office (myself, Eve Holroyd as the booking agent, and another assistant) decided on an ultramodern teak look. One wall was covered in purple felt with appliquéd flowers. The public relations people, Roger Cowles and Gaby Sturmer, decided on a rich antique look with Canaletto-painted wallpaper and leather covered desks.

The last "office" or space was devoted to the inspirational team: graphic design and branding. Hamish Grimes, a longtime Giorgio friend, was the designer (his brother Michael was a set designer who also designed the offices).

The reception was ultra bright white, and Angie Driscoll was the receptionist. She was ably assisted by a parrot called Peckaboo. I remember listening on the telephone to tracks the Yardbirds had laid down at Sun Records in Memphis, and we all knew they had a number one record. We were all very excited. The Yardbirds' success meant that there had to be someone to keep up with the fan mail.

One young woman came to our office to answer the letters, many of which requested any kind of memento. We began saving cigarette butts and locks of hair to send.

By then, in addition to the Yardbirds, we were managing Gary Farr and the T-Bones, Julie Driscoll, Brian Auger, and others I cannot recall. Giorgio lost management of the Rolling Stones to Andrew Loog Oldham in 1963 when he returned to Italy/Switzerland to bury his father. During that time, the Stones, who were part of the Crawdaddy Club groups Giorgio organized, signed the Oldham agreement.

In conjunction with Polydor Records, who had hired Frank Fenter from one of the music publishing companies, Paragon was to prepare and arrange press conferences for all Stax/Volt artists, released via Atlantic Records and distributed through Polydor. Fenter developed a close relationship during that time with Ahmet and Nesuhi Ertegun at Atlantic.

Other groups signed up for media relations, including the Moody Blues, Eric Burdon and the Animals, the Soft Machine, and maybe Cream, but I cannot remember.

We started our own recording label called Marmalade Records, which I managed and which was distributed via

Polydor. We released records by artists including Julie Driscoll, Brian Auger and the Trinity, and Blossom Toes, as well as recordings by Graham Gouldman, Kevin Godley, Eric Stewart, and Lol Crème before they became 10cc.

The joint release of the Bob Dylan song "This Wheel's on Fire" by Julie Driscoll and Brian Auger and the Trinity reached number five in England in 1968.

Our first release was a controversial single called "We Love the Pirates" in August 1966. The musicians were well known, mostly musicians of the Ivy League who would later call themselves the Flower Pot Men, but they did it under the pseudonym of the Roaring 60s. Radio Caroline, Radio London, and Radio 270 gave it extensive airplay, but the single did not become a hit.

The Marmalade label ceased to exist in 1969 when Polydor stopped financing Giorgio's venture. To celebrate Polydor's 50th anniversary, Paragon Publicity and PR teamed up with Polydor Europe for an extravaganza in Montreux, Switzerland. We had the entire Casino at our disposal. We rented a Dutch mime group and models, we showed Jimi Hendrix's movie, we covered an entire wall with aluminum foil and projected oils onto it. There was a palm court quartet and bouncy balls, and it was one evening of extreme fun.

We also arranged to have the entire stage production of *Hair* appear in Montreux. The logistics were all up to me, including inviting the police chief from Lausanne so he could convince himself that this was not a lewd porn show. Big success. Again, I think this must have been in 1969.

While Giorgio's visions might have driven a few people bonkers, it was my pleasure to facilitate any strange request. Such was the case when Frank Zappa appeared at the Albert Hall. Giorgio wanted a tutu (which he got), and Zappa wanted a really large Rank gong, which he got. (What I had no clue about, thankfully, was that there was a gaggle of call girls that entertained the groups after hours, literally).

I was the sane, organized, straight one. No drugs (gin fizz). I cooked for the groups on weekends, and we'd end up on some green somewhere playing soccer.

Once, Aretha Franklin, Otis Redding, Sam and Dave and others appeared as they prepared for their tours. We also met the people from their management in the US.

When Otis died in 1967, he was better known than Elvis, and news of his death meant we were called to come up with any footage of his stage shows. The one we had access to is now available online, *Otis Redding Live in Paris*. His manager, Phil Walden, sat in my office before Otis died and talked in that strange southern drawl about music in the US.

We also set up the opening celebrations for the Speakeasy Club, with Jimi Hendrix and many others just grooving away and eating shrimp-stuffed avocados. The club scene was very much part of what we did. We arrived at work around ten in the morning, knocked off at five or six, went home, and then reappeared at a club around ten in the evening.

Frank Fenter's old boss was Ian Ralfini. He decided to open an office for MGM, and in the autumn (I think) of 1969 I left Giorgio and the increasingly complicated world of Polydor/Paragon/Marmalade. I joined MGM as an A&R manager, only to be foiled by the continuous change of leadership at MGM in the US, meaning we had to rerelease Connie Francis over and over (yuck, sorry).

Giorgio left as well. He went to Paris and the rest ..."

***

During my correspondence with Madeleine Carr, she suggested I contact Brian Godding whose wife Angie was Julie Driscoll's sister. Brian was a founding member of

Blossom Toes, the band for which he also wrote their best-known songs, including "Kiss of Confusion".

Brian Godding's early influences included the Shadows, the Beatles, Bo Diddley, Chuck Berry, and Jimi Hendrix. He started playing guitar in a band called the Gravediggers. After renaming themselves the Ingoes, the band played in the local clubs of London and decided to look for a manager. The only one they could find was Giorgio Gomelsky, who was managing the Yardbirds and the Crawdaddy Club in Richmond, but Giorgio told them to come back and see him when they had improved their act.

During the winter of 1964, the band decided to follow the trail of many other English bands – the one that led to Germany, more particularly to a club in the town of Dortmund. There, they played for a crowd of British soldiers and German rockers who did not really mix with each other, and the Ingoes did their best to satisfy everybody with songs like "Skinny Minnie," "Route 66," and "Johnny B. Goode," which they performed in half-hour sets six times per night. His most pleasant memory from those days is meeting up with the

other musicians, who were all going through the same learning process under this gruelling performing schedule.

Back in England, they went to see the "dragon" – Giorgio, but the "gorgon" was still not impressed. However, he appreciated the

Brian Godding at the BBC, 1969.

experience they had gained on their German tour and he asked his assistant Hamish Grimes to find them the kind of work that would improve their act, and that was how they became Sonny Boy Williamson's backup band playing in various seedy clubs around South London. Brian found it challenging working with Sonny Boy, whose bad temper was legendary, and he decided to give up playing the blues under those conditions.

After that, the Ingoes played a few gigs in other clubs closer to the centre of London – including the Marquee. Giorgio finally thought they were ready and offered them a management contract, and the band suddenly arrived at the Crawdaddy as the opening act for the Yardbirds, the Moody Blues, and the T-Bones.

Brian sent me his memories of Giorgio from London by email on August 17, 2017:

"As you will appreciate, fitting Giorgio into a nutshell would be nigh on impossible. :-)

Was he a friend of mine? Simple answer is 'yes'.

Did I respect him? Of course. Anybody who could converse in multiple languages without blinking an eye deserves respect, don't they?

Did I trust him? One grew to accept (trust) that his intentions (visions) were good though not always achievable in reality but generally enlightening and exciting to be part of in most cases.

Did I like him? Very much. His strength of character and vulnerability as a human being were well-defined in life, and for me, this simplified and stabilized our friendship (nobody is perfect).

So Giorgio was a friend of mine for sure, and I think I was one of his."

"David (Aellen) was kind of a polyglot. He was Australian.
He came to Europe on a Greek ship as a stowaway. And
then they found him out, and they took his guitars, and he
started singing them songs, and they said OK and gave
him a ticket from Athens to Paris ..."
– GOMELSKY

Daevid Allen on stage in Hyde Park with Gong,
June 1974. Photo: Tim Duncan

7. PARIS: SOFT MACHINE, GONG, AND MAGMA

"All these people came to see me because I was the only one who spoke languages. And that's how it started. I went to Paris to do my own thing, and I met this girl, and she became my wife." – GOMELSKY

During Giorgio's "French years", I was in South America living thousands of miles away in the Amazon jungle and Rio de Janeiro, and the music that Giorgio had produced in France was completely unknown to me.

Moreover, as soon as I arrived in New York, survival had forced me to make choices that had nothing to do with the culture of the underground, and it was four years before I would meet Giorgio and start getting back in the groove of the music culture I had once known and loved.

Our friendship became stronger with time, but our conversations rarely focused on his life and activities in France. Something seemed to hold him back and I did not want to press him. But he was obviously proud of the work he had done with Soft Machine, Gong, and Magma.

Daevid Allen was a guitar and bass player from Australia who moved to London in 1961, where he started the band Soft Machine in 1966 (named after a book written by William S. Burroughs), with Robert Wyatt on drums, Kevin Ayers on bass, and Mike Ratledge on keyboards. Giorgio saw them play at the UFO Club, and he invited them to record demos for an album in 1967. But much to his chagrin, Polydor showed no interest.

He offered Soft Machine a tour in France, which ended in Saint-Tropez for a series of concerts, but when the band returned to England, Daevid Allen, an Australian, was turned away by British immigration officers. Daevid stayed behind in Paris, where he started the band Gong with his partner Gillian Mary Smyth. When Giorgio moved to Paris in 1969, he became their manager and got them a contract with BYG Actuel records for their first LP, *Magick Brother,* produced in 1970 by Jean Georgakarakos and Jean-Luc Young. Daevid Allen played the bass guitar on this record, instead of Christian Tritsch, who could not make the session.

Following their second and third LPs on BYG and Philips, Giorgio got them a recording contract for three LPs with Virgin Records, Richard Branson's new record label. He also produced the first two of their three LPs, *Flying Teapot* and *Angel's Egg,* both in 1973. When Daevid Allen and Gill Smyth left the band in 1975, Giorgio departed as

Gong performing in Hyde Park, 1974. Photo: Tim Duncan

their manager too.

In the same period, Giorgio became the manager of another band called Magma. He often told me that Magma was his favourite among all the bands he'd managed. He discovered them at a concert he had gone to a bit reluctantly in 1970, shortly after his arrival from England, at a time when he wanted to avoid the music industry and focus again on his filmmaking career.

A crowd of 200 people was at the concert, and Giorgio had been very impressed by the quality of the music and the talent of the musicians. He said in an interview:

> "I had never heard anything like it. I was very impressed by their "sources" and their musical skills. This was not run-of-the-mill stuff. It also wasn't "commercial" by any stretch of the imagination. But I'm a sucker for underdogs, so I was tempted to take on the challenge."[1]

With his connections, he was able to secure them a recording contract with Philips which released their first two LPs in 1970 and 1971, *Magma* and *1001° Centigrades* – *Magma* being a double LP.

In 1973 and 1974, Giorgio produced their third and fifth LPs: *Mëkanïk Dëstruktïw Kömmandöh* and *Köhntarkösz* for Vertigo Records. With Giorgio's help, Magma managed to give sixty concerts a year for crowds which quickly grew from a few hundred to around 3,000 people per concert, and to sell 150,000 LPs in France alone.

One day, he went to a local youth centre (MJC) to meet with Klaus Blasquiz, the lead vocalist of Magma, who was teaching art there. Since he was early and had to wait a while, he looked around and saw that the place had a small stage with a space for an audience of about two hundred people. Giorgio asked to see the manager and found out that nobody actually used the space. He immediately offered to produce

---

1   Giorgio Gomelsky interview www.eurock.com/features/giorgio.aspx

a concert there with no upfront financial guarantees, but with the offer of 15 percent of the box office revenue for the venue *if* Giorgio could use the photocopy machine to print flyers for free.

The manager accepted, and Giorgio began promoting his new concert right away. The circuit for bands playing in the Student Unions of universities in the United Kingdom was well-established, and Giorgio recognised the opportunity to set up a similar circuit in French youth centres and universities. He discovered that there were about two hundred youth centres with small theatres that nobody used, and he began phoning around the venues. Twenty-five of them accepted his offer and two weeks later, Magma started its first tour of youth centres, giving five concerts a week for five weeks.

This proved an ideal network to use to tour the new bands he was promoting. The venue administrators were happy to earn hire fees and the young audiences were keen to hear new sounds and new acts. Giorgio drew in the crowds and grew the audiences and fans for his bands by word of mouth, weekly. The immediate result was that the bands that played live on this circuit quickly improved their skills and also made a little money, enough for the musicians to give up their day jobs.

Gong was interested in joining this network too, and in 1973 they started Rock Pas Dégénéré (Rock Not Degenerate), an agency for progressive rock musicians that became the largest of its kind in Europe, with more than a hundred concerts a year. German, Dutch, and English bands joined this network for their tours, which also gave French bands a chance to tour other European countries as a sort of cultural exchange.

As if this wasn't enough to keep him busy, Giorgio was also working with other bands, like the English avant-garde rock band Henry Cow, and German groups that started the krautrock movement such as Amon Düül II and Can, and he also helped Vangelis to produce his album *666* for Aphrodite's Child at the end of 1970 and beginning of 1971.

Once again, Giorgio seemed to be a catalyst for change and innovation and he found himself at the forefront of the development of avant-garde music in France and Germany.

When Giorgio decided to go to the States in 1977, Magma was giving close to a hundred concerts a year, earning from $5,000 to $10,000 per concert. The last Magma concert that Giorgio went to was when they opened for Léo Ferré, who had invited them to play under a huge circus tent for an audience of 5,000 people.

Unlike many promoters and managers in the music industry, money was not the main driver for Giorgio. He could be described as a kind of influencer, or impresario, who liked to enable musicians and bands to build a loyal

Magma c.1974

following, not only those he was managing. The gig circuit he created allowed many French and European bands to develop their skills and their fanbase too. This concept and altruistic attitude were rewarded with free and positive feedback from the press.

He believed in this principle: If the prophet goes to the mountain, the mountain will return the favour a hundredfold. In spite of a marked resistance from the conservative government of Georges Pompidou towards such events, Giorgio made friends and allies in other French political organizations which had their own venues and regular events. The Fêtes de l'Huma – the huge annual parties given by the French Communist paper *L'Humanité* – were also important gigs for Magma, which played at the festival every year in front of huge crowds.

By decentralizing the traditional network run by the established musical institutions, Giorgio realized his dream of complete and real democratization of the system to give each and every band an equal chance to be known, seen, and heard. Whenever he mentioned this highly productive period of his life, he spoke of it fondly.

But everything comes to an end. Christian Vander, the drummer and founder of Magma, and Jannik Top, the composer and bass player, broke up at the end of 1976, just before Magma were about to undertake an important three-week tour in England. Giorgio decided to depart as their manager, at this point too, and to focus on his new record label, Utopia, which he was developing with RCA, and this was what brought him to New York.

Giorgio had been happy for a time in Paris. He had married a concert producer, Brigitte Guichard, who organised the first tour for Pink Floyd in France. They also had a daughter, named Donatella. I had the pleasure of meeting Brigitte at Christmas in 1984 in Paris, when I took a present to her on behalf of Giorgio.

Giorgio was always very private about family matters and I didn't pry into the reasons for the break up of his relationships. If he suffered from the estrangement with his family, he didn't show it, but perhaps this was what drove him to create a new community of artists and musicians around him, wherever he went.

Twenty years later, musicians that Giorgio had worked with in Paris were still dropping in to see him whenever they came to New York. His daughter Donatella often visited him in the school holidays too, and she would later move to New York to study film, and settle in the USA.

Giorgio sometimes told me that he did miss his family, and the French friends and musicians he had grown close to, particularly those in Gong and Magma, but the charm of Paris could not match the irresistible appeal and energy of life in New York.

With Magma, we were very organized, you could trust Christian to be there. And they loved rehearsals, and they were working and working ... and no ganja, no cocaine..." – GOMELSKY

Christian Vander of Magma c.1975

"When I came to New York in '78 ... I saw all these people who were searching for things here, and they wanted me to bring this underground music, this avant-garde music from Europe..." – GOMELSKY

Das Fürlines were a punk rock band in New York in the 1980s. Members included Holly Hemlock (guitar, vocals), Deb O'Nair (keyboards, vocals, accordion), Liz Luv (bass guitar), Wendy Wild (vocals, banjo, guitar) and Rachel Schnitzel (drums)

8. NEW YORK AND THE HOUSE AT 140 WEST 24TH STREET

In 1976, RCA offered Giorgio a lucrative contract to open a new label, Utopia Records, which he wanted to transform into some kind of headquarters for the worldwide cultural underground, and this brought him to New York regularly for contractual meetings with lawyers.

The agreement with RCA was one of the most profitable deals that Giorgio ever made, but as so often happened in the music business, his other business partners could not be relied upon to deliver, which led to frequent business meetings to discuss contractual obligations. Between his appointments, Giorgio liked to walk around the city, exploring its diverse neighbourhoods, and the energy and cultural life seduced him a little more each time he visited. He finally decided to move to New York at the end of 1977. He liked to joke that he had walked around the town so much that he had worn out his wooden clogs.

Finally, RCA offered him a consulting job, and thanks to the money he received from this new contract, he took a room at the Gramercy Park Hotel, before moving to a large apartment in a luxury condominium building located at 21 West 16th Street, which he could easily afford with the monthly salary of 5,000 dollars that he received from RCA.

He regularly visited New York clubs like CBGB, the Village Gate, the Bitter End, the Bottom Line, and Max's

Kansas City, where he met musicians including Bill Laswell, who would move into his house later on.

However, his plans for the Utopia Records project crumbled and he soon had a cash flow problem which meant paying the rent was difficult. Moreover, Giorgio and his musician friends made too much noise for the landlord, who happened to live in the building. He had to find another place. Casting around the neighbourhood, he found a house at 140 West 24th Street with a large basement area. He moved in during the spring of 1978, and quickly opened what he named The Zu Club.

When they first met, Bill Laswell was only 24 years old, and Giorgio soon encouraged him to start a band, which he allowed to rehearse in the basement of the house. Bill would also move into a room on the second floor for a while. The band he formed took the name the Zu Band and Giorgio introduced them to Daevid Allen of Gong. This led to a new band that played under the name of New York Gong for an event that Giorgio created and organized, which he called the Zu New Music Manifestival. (The name was derived from two ideas – "Zu" is the name of an ancient Egyptian messenger bird, and "Mani" is the root of the word "manifesto.")

Giorgio financed the event himself with the 3,000 dollars advance that he had received from the London office of Charly Records for a new Gong album.

On October 8, 1978, around a thousand people turned up at New York's Entermedia Theatre, which is located at the corner of

Bill Laswell c.1981

Second Avenue and East 12th Street, for a unique show that lasted 14 hours, with improvised performances from around 70 US and European musicians.

Some of the artists taking part included the French drummer François Laizeau, the percussionist Chris Cutler and the guitar player Fred Frith of the band Henry Cow, the Hungarian band Neffesh-Music, led by the sax player Yochk'o Seffer, and, topping the bill, the Australian Daevid Allen, who had founded Soft Machine and Gong.

The event was a huge success which went on all night until the police forced the theatre owner to switch the power off at four in the morning. Despite this, some of the musicians continued to play acoustically in the dark with the huge audience cheering them on. Finally, they all spilled out onto the street at dawn, where the mood for dancing carried on. The police were seriously annoyed by the disturbance it had caused but Giorgio was delighted by the success of the event and the positive response of those involved.

However, despite its cultural and artistic value, this musical experiment was a unique one-off. The musicians who took part actually lost money, and the project, no matter how commendable, was a financial disaster.

Following a brief tour in France, the musicians of the New York Gong band broke up with Daevid Allen and returned to New York. Bill Laswell was among those who started a new band called Material and they recorded the instrumental album *Temporary Music* for Giorgio's Zu Records label, which was distributed by Celluloid.

Giorgio thought that it would be a good idea to try and get a gig circuit going as he had done with the youth centres in France, and in March of 1979, he took two dozen musicians on a school bus for a three month tour across the United States, playing over thirty venues. However, he had not appreciated the vast distances involved to travel between the concert venues nor the enormous differences in beliefs and attitudes between communities, with the people living in the Midwest generally far more conservative than those living in the urban areas. The experience taught him that America was way too big and culturally diverse to be able to create the same kind of youth network as he had initiated in France. Nor was he able to build an audience by word of mouth and with different radio stations serving each state, it was challenging to get media attention for his new band, Zu.

In Los Angeles, he tried to create another Zu New Music Manifestival similar to the one he had successfully organized in New York the year before, but the tour and the Los Angeles event both made a big loss.

Whereas others might have given up, Giorgio shrugged it off. His main regret was that he had not documented the tour on video, as it produced several remarkable moments. His belief that he had to think on a global scale while acting on a local level, even if things did not always work out as planned, was ahead of his time. He would say that change was the only constant in the universe, even if the thought of change is frightening.

***

Steve Marriott, centre, & the Small Faces, 1966

Giorgio was still living in the house at 140 West 24th Street, eight years later, but he did not own it. A verbal agreement with his old partners led him to believe that they would eventually sign over the deeds to him, but it never happened. Although they had bought the house, and promised him the sky, he was only ever a tenant there.

By 1986, the house was in a dilapidated state. It was virtually uninhabitable and Giorgio had become depressed. Few of his old musician friends dropped in and hardly any bands came to rehearse in the basement. A stray black and white cat moved in. Every morning it would drop the mice it had killed during the night outside Giorgio's apartment door. To thank it, Giorgio would feed it, leaving a bowl of cat food on the ground floor every afternoon.

Even a visit from Steve Marriott, one of the founders of the Small Faces, who Giorgio had known well in London, did not manage to change his gloomy mood. He was obviously happy to see Steve, but nothing really seemed to bring back his lust for life, which I knew so well. I wanted to see him get his mojo back – to hear his voice loud and clear and see his eyes sparkle. But Giorgio was suffering from a midlife crisis, where the slights and rip offs he had endured rankled with him, and a feeling of bitterness had emerged.

Giorgio would constantly complain about how the original Yardbirds' tapes had been copied and reissued as pirate recordings, without his consent. The pirated records were made in Mexico, and the sleeves were printed in Poland, while the sales revenue disappeared into ghost bank accounts, that made it untraceable.

Finally, in 1986, he accepted a few tens of thousands of dollars as a final settlement for the rights to reproduce the Yardbirds' tapes. As he was in desperate need of money, he accepted the deal outright, without having the foresight to realise that the new medium of CDs would give these recordings a new lease of life. This was an impulsive choice which cost him dearly, but his view was that the popularity of these recordings would diminish in time, in keeping with the ever-changing trends and volatility of the music business.

Two years after he sold his rights away, a 4 CD box set was released, one of the very first of its kind. It included Eric Clapton's *Crossroads*, which enjoyed a phenomenal international success. Four million copies were sold, and it won four awards, including two Grammys. The first nine songs of the first CD were tracks recorded by the Yardbirds and produced by Giorgio Gomelsky, who unfortunately never received a single penny from it.

On September 7, 2011, a new lineup of the Yardbirds gave a concert at the BB King's Blues Club located at 237 West 42nd Street, near Times Square. Chris Dreja and Jim McCarty, the only two original members left in the band, called Giorgio and invited him to join them for an interview that would promote their current American tour on WOR, a New York radio station.

Giorgio was excited to be included in the interview, but this did little to help improve the dire situation he was in financially. Although he knew this, the call of his old musician friends and partners, and the fact that they had invited him in the first place, made him extremely happy.

9. MEETING GIORGIO

"They didn't call it rock then. In London they called it rhythm 'n' blues." – GOMELSKY

When I visited England for the first time in March-April 1963, the Beatles were creating a buzz with their single "Please Please Me" which led me to explore the record shops. I soon realized that the way LPs were pressed in the UK offered a much better aural quality than their French equivalents. As I was a fan of the Shadows, I started to buy their records in England from that first trip onwards, and I carried on doing this for years as I extended my collection of American and English blues/rock.

On June 20, 1965, I went to the afternoon concert of the Beatles at the Palais des Sports in Paris. My father had managed to get me two seats in the middle of the front row, the best seats in the house. The audience went wild when the Beatles came on stage and it was impossible to hear much of the music, with all the screaming girls in the audience. Although seeing the Beatles was exciting, I preferred watching and listening to the Yardbirds (with Jeff Beck). They opened the show and, for me, it was a more interesting musical experience.

Little did I know that Giorgio was standing backstage at that concert. It was thanks to his relationship with Brian Epstein, who managed the Beatles, that the Yardbirds were the support act, not only in Paris but throughout the Beatles'

Ticket for the Beatles concert in Paris, June 20, 1965

tour of Europe in the spring of 1965.

I would never have guessed then that Giorgio and I would become friends fifteen years later, and that our friendship would last for more than thirty years. In 1987, we shared our memories of this concert – with him backstage, and me in the middle of the front row. He told me that the Yardbirds had played for longer than they were supposed to, and that while waiting for their turn to go on stage, the Beatles were joking, "Do you think they're going to let us play today?"

I spent two months in England ten days after this memorable concert. Like many teens of the time, I liked the international hit "For Your Love," which the Yardbirds released in March 1965 in the UK and in April 1965 in the US. During my summer holidays in England, I started looking for record stores that specialized in blues and rock music. That's how I found *Five Live Yardbirds*, the LP produced by Giorgio at the Marquee Club in London on March 20, 1964.

The following year, I discovered the album of Sonny Boy Williamson backed by the Animals and recorded at the Club A'Gogo in Newcastle on December 30, 1963. This record was also produced by Giorgio Gomelsky, whose name became my standard of quality for the type of music I enjoyed the most.

Back in Paris, I started to buy the weekly English pop culture magazines, where I read that Giorgio's name was linked to many musicians such as the Rolling Stones and the Beatles in what was now called Swingin' London.

Reading the information in the music magazines, I learned that Giorgio had been the first manager of the Rolling Stones, when they started playing weekly in his club, the Crawdaddy, located in Richmond, Surrey. Due to his relationship with Brian Epstein, Giorgio had introduced the Stones to John Lennon and Paul McCartney. The meeting led to their song "I Wanna Be Your Man" being recorded by the Stones three weeks before the Beatles released their version of the song on the LP, *With the Beatles* in UK (and *Meet the Beatles* in US), with Ringo on lead vocals. The Rolling Stones released their version on their second single on November 1, 1963, with a great slide guitar solo by Brian Jones, who had mastered the Elmore James technique better than any other British musician in those days. Brian Jones had even gone by the nickname of Elmo Lewis, his full name being Lewis Brian Hopkin Jones.

Epstein appeared on many TV programmes and was a regular host of the American TV show *Hullabaloo*. Giorgio and Brian Epstein continued to collaborate until Brian's death on August 27, 1967 by which time the Beatles were going in different directions and would split in 1970.

During the mid-60s, Giorgio continued to make hits with the Yardbirds, with Jeff Beck replacing Eric Clapton on lead guitar. However, in 1966, I realized that Giorgio was no longer their producer, as this role had been taken over by their bass player, Paul Samwell-Smith. Chris Dreja had subsequently moved to bass guitar from playing rhythm

GIORGIO GOMELSKY 'FOR YOUR LOVE'

The Yardbirds perform for the film *Blow Up,* 1966

guitar in the group.

Finally, Jimmy Page joined the band and we can see him playing lead guitar in the scene of the movie *Blow-Up*, which Michelangelo Antonioni directed in 1966. In the film, Jeff Beck destroys a guitar prop in the style of Pete Townshend of the Who, the band which had been the first choice of the director for this scene of destruction. It is worth noting that it was Jimmy Page who played bass on the audio track although he was shown playing lead guitar in the actual film.

The song, "Stroll On," was actually a version of "The Train Kept a-Rollin'," which Giorgio had produced in Memphis at Sam Phillips' Sun Studio, with different lyrics for copyright reasons. Then Peter Grant's name appeared as manager and Giorgio's time with the Yardbirds was over.

The band released several recordings in 1967, but their popularity was in decline. They finally toured the United States for the last time, and a farewell concert was recorded at the Anderson Theatre in New York on March 30, 1968. However, shortly after the release of the album, featuring early versions of "White Summer" and the long blues "I'm Confused," which would both be recorded later by Led Zeppelin, Peter Grant took it out of distribution at the request of Jimmy Page. The album then became a rare gem for bootleggers and collectors.

The band broke up, and new musicians were considered, including the drummer Keith Moon, who was thinking of leaving the Who and who came up with the name Lead Zeppelin, which Jimmy Page changed to Led Zeppelin. The writing was on the wall, the final curtain came down on the Yardbirds, and Giorgio's name disappeared from my radar.

***

I left France in 1971 and spent six years in South America before moving to New York, where I decided to settle. I began producing cable television programs in 1979 – before the existence of CNN and MTV – and started my own company, Get It On TV, with prime time programs that were shown on Manhattan Cable Television five nights a week. The *New York Times* considered me a pioneer of cable television in a long article published on February 12, 1980 about this burgeoning industry.

When I first met Giorgio at his house at 140 West 24th Street, we immediately had a good rapport. I went to see him with Ronnie Bird, on the recommendation of our mutual friend Nicole Devilaine, to exchange ideas about new technologies, the use of satellites, and cable television.

Giorgio had a very charismatic personality, spoke with a nondescript Russian accent, and could be charming at times or imposing at others. When he suggested that we should launch a bunch of satellites into the stratosphere to start an international communications network that would be free from any governmental control, I wasn't keen to get involved. I had just been forced to close my TV company, after making a financial loss, and I could not see how we were going to start up this multimillion-dollar venture without any investors.

Giorgio told me about his new record company, named Guillotine Records. The company logo depicted a few drops of blood under the slogan "A Cut Above the Rest"– an obvious play on words. He gave me a copy of his latest record by the band A Blind Dog Stares.

Bill Laswell had been living in Giorgio's house and had, by then, started the band Material, with Giorgio producing several tracks for their first album. Bill had progressed to becoming the in-house producer for Celluloid Records, a New York record label founded by Jean Karakos, who knew Giorgio from his days in Paris, where they had worked together with the bands Gong and Magma. Their relationship did not end well, but Giorgio gave me a contact at Celluloid Records whose offices were on 81st Street and Central Park West.

I left Giorgio's house with Ronnie as the sun was shining on the streets of New York. My first venture with French TV and my first meeting with Giorgio opened a beautiful new chapter in my life, and with youthful optimism, it seemed that everything was possible from then on.

I called the office of Celluloid. Jean Karakos was out of town, but his assistant invited me to come and meet her. She gave me copies of records their office was trying to promote in the United States so that I could become familiar with their roster of artists, such as the band Etron Fou Leloublan. She also gave me the contact numbers of Dominique Farran at RTL (Radio Télé Luxembourg) in Paris so that I could meet with him next time I went back to Paris.

When she came to New York a few months later, I met Michèle Halberstadt, who had her own show on Radio 7 in Paris, and I introduced her to Giorgio. She improvised an interview on her small portable tape recorder, with the hope that it would help revive Giorgio's flame in France. Michèle had been recommended to me by Dominique Farran, whom I had met in Paris a few weeks earlier.

I saw Giorgio more and more often and we realized that we were interested in similar topics. When I told him of my master's thesis, which I wrote about Jack Kerouac and the Beat Generation for my university in Paris in 1971, Giorgio asked me to give him a copy. He read it, was interested, and asked me if I would consider writing his biography. I was pleasantly surprised and happy to accept, but I quickly discovered that working with him was nearly impossible: vague promises, no contract, no distribution, and no deadline for a book that seemed to be more of a distant dream than an actual project.

It was around this time that I heard that Ahmet Ertegun, the chairman and cofounder of Atlantic Records, had invited Giorgio to manage the American branch of Polydor Records, a European label that was considering being distributed by Warner Bros. in the States. It would have

Ahmet Ertegun and his brother, Nesuhi. c.1960. Photo: LoC

required Giorgio to give up his bohemian lifestyle and switch to a more corporate approach with regular office hours and a business discipline that Ahmet had mastered brilliantly. Inevitably, it fell through, and their relationship never recovered.

Later on, Ahmet Ertegun became the founder of the Rock and Roll Hall of Fame, which started accepting names to be considered for the first awards to be given on January 23, 1986. First and foremost, the candidates had to be artists, but a special annual award was created to recognize those who had been influential in the development of artistic careers, such as managers, producers, promoters, etc.

The first two of these special awards were given to Alan Freed and Sam Phillips, followed later on by Leonard Chess, Ahmet Ertegun, Andrew Loog Oldham, and Brian Epstein – all Giorgio's contemporaries, whom he knew quite well and with whom he had worked. But regrettably, Giorgio himself has yet to be recognized. Moreover, this special award was named 'The Ahmet Ertegun Award', which meant that candidates for the award had to have his blessing. Who knows if Giorgio will ever be the posthumous recipient of this award, now that he and Ahmet have both passed away?

Although the biography project had been on the back burner for many years, I decided to write this book because Giorgio deserves recognition for his significant contribution to the development of international rock and roll music.

In December 1980 and January 1981, the movie *Downtown 81* was partially filmed in Giorgio's house, but it took forever to find a distributor, and it was only released in 2000 on a very small scale. The main part was played by the artist Jean-Michel Basquiat, who is portrayed as renting an apartment in Giorgio's house. This was at a time when Basquiat was an impoverished artist and couldn't pay his rent so Giorgio plays the character of a landlord who is trying to get him evicted. Giorgio was always interested in art and if he had acquired one of Basquiat's paintings from that time, the rest of his life might have been easier.

On September 19, 1981, I visited Giorgio to ask him if he'd like to come with me to Central Park for the free Simon and Garfunkel concert. The City of New York estimated that a crowd of half a million people was expected. He was not keen on joining such a large crowd, and he had set up a TV set and a fantastic sound system to watch the concert quietly at home.

I waved goodbye and went to the entrance of Central Park at Fifth Avenue and 76th Street, only to find that the crowd was so huge that I could not even get inside the park. I ended up going home to watch the concert on TV as well.

My friend Patrick Kurtkowiak came to spend two weeks in New York in September 1981, just as he had done the year before. But this time, he came with a small budget to record four songs he had written, which he hoped to distribute in Paris. Patrick asked me to find him some musicians and a recording studio.

I called my friend Chris, and we had a guitarist. Chris called Gary, and we had a bassist. Then I called Giorgio, who recommended Sami, the French drummer of the Volcanos, a rock band from the Lower East Side. The band was now complete with Patrick as the singer. I named our new group the French Fries.

Of course we rehearsed at Giorgio's, who rented us some studio space in the house at 140 West 24th Street. The basement, the ground floor, and the first floor were more or less soundproof, but it was unbearably hot, in spite of the huge fans. We learned the four songs and I booked A1, a recording studio that I picked at random from reading the *Village Voice* ads.

It transpired that this was Herb Abramson's recording

studio. He had co-founded Atlantic Records with Ahmet Ertegun in 1947. His wife Miriam had been in charge of administrative duties, while Ahmet and Herb were in charge of the music production. After a number of artistic differences, Herb left ATCO and eventually started A1 Sound Studios, which was based in the building of the Beacon Theatre at Broadway and 75th Street.

Herb himself produced the four tracks in one day, and he even gave Patrick's voice a country rock tone, which surprised us pleasantly. However, Patrick did not manage to successfully find distribution for the recordings when he returned to Paris. In September, 1982 he came back to New York with two more songs and hooked up with Chris and Gary again, but we needed a new drummer, since Sami had moved back to France. Gary recruited one of his friends, and we rehearsed once again at Giorgio's house, as well as on the stage of a club called Black Beans, that Giorgio had just opened on the same block of West 24th Street, and that he managed from his apartment.

In July of 1982, Nicole Devilaine called me to say that Jean-Pierre Elkabbach was coming to New York and that he was interested in meeting me to talk about my experience as a Cable TV producer. Jean-Pierre had run the news department of Antenne 2 in Paris. Cable TV had not yet seen the light of day in France, and he wanted to be a part of its development when it was eventually rolled out.

I had met the man before and I knew him to be very conservative in both his style and thinking. Since I did not know what to do to entertain him after our meeting, I thought of taking him to Tramps, a nightclub near Union Square where Giorgio regularly produced events.

Giorgio had already produced his Tonka Wonka nights at the Bitter End at 147 Bleecker Street, the Greenwich Village club that had developed a good reputation and following since the days when Bob Dylan had played there in 1961. Having produced variety nights at Tramps, where he acted as the in-house DJ, he brought the concept of his Tonka Wonka Mondays there. I invited Jean-Pierre Elkabbach to come along and enjoy the music of a Haitian rock-reggae band that was topping the bill, and we spent a fantastic night there thanks to the great hospitality of Giorgio Gomelsky.

The idea of these Tonka Wonka nights was highly original. Giorgio would bring together musicians who played jazz, rock, and/or world music to play in front of a group of professional critics, and the evening would end with a performance by whichever group had the top billing of the night.

This proved highly popular, and the house at 140 West 24th St. was no longer big enough to welcome all the bands that wanted to rehearse there. He also started to produce plays there for small audiences of about fifty people which created a unique New York City atmosphere.

In 1982, Giorgio had a new idea to develop a musical hip-hop show that would be the first of its kind. The producer Joseph Papp, who ran the Public Theatre in the old building of the Astor Library in Manhattan, agreed to explore this possibility in his theatre, and Giorgio got the support of various artists and producers, like Futura 2000, Mr. Freeze, and Lori Eastside, as well as composers like Dave Soldier and Mark Mazur of the band Kid Creole and the Coconuts. But in spite of the high quality of all involved, this project fell apart and never saw the light of day.

Giorgio's parties became more and more the talk of the town in New York's underground milieu. There was a continuous parade of musicians, actors, producers, and freeloaders, but money continued to be hard to come by.

In 1983, I started a band that I called the United Notions because we were truly international: I'm French, the two percussionists were Brazilian, the drummer was Japanese, and the lead guitarist and the bass player were both American.

I rented some rehearsal space on the ground floor at Giorgio's place and we publicised the gig locally. We soon sold out and I went on to organise more successful gigs there for other bands, which Giorgio appreciated because the income helped to keep the house running, something that was becoming increasingly difficult for him.

The building at 140 West 24th Street was a large property with four floors and Giorgio lived in the loft on the top floor. He got the lease to the house in 1978 from people in the fashion business who stored mannequins for designers and runway shows. When Ronnie Bird met with Giorgio again in New York, it was he who restored the top floor. The basement was rented as rehearsal space to a band on a monthly basis, the ground floor was the main social space where there was a stage set up for bands to play, and there was a rehearsal studio on the second floor that could be

Giorgio as bartender at one of his private parties, 1994

MEETING GIORGIO

Laswell at Moers Festival, 2006. Photo: Michael Hoefner

rented for $20 per hour.

There was also a room on the second floor where Bill Laswell used to sleep before finding fame with his band Material, and before his work with Mick Jagger for the production of Jagger's first solo album, *She's the Boss.*

This room was later the home of another musician, Scott MacAuley.

Scotty did everything for Giorgio. He was a young and friendly American who, besides being an excellent musician in his own right, was also an expert at repairing amplifiers, drum kits, PA systems, and other instruments that needed constant care. During the 80s the house was also known for a time as the Plugg Club which catered for lovers of No Wave music.

Another memorable night was December 9, 1983, when a charity concert for A.R.M.S. (Action into Research for Multiple Sclerosis) was organised by Ronnie Lane, who was a victim of MS himself.

This event brought Eric Clapton, Jeff Beck, and Jimmy Page – the three legendary guitar players of the Yardbirds from Giorgio Gomelsky's time – onto the same stage at Madison Square Garden for the first time ever.

The rhythm section featured Charlie Watts and Bill Wyman of the Rolling Stones, plus Kenney Jones of the Who and the percussionist Ray Cooper. Steve Winwood sang and played the organ, Ronnie Wood played guitar, and Joe Cocker was as impressive as ever on vocals, with a little help from his friends, such as John Paul Jones and Andy Fairweather Low.

When Jimmy Page walked on stage and played the instrumental part of "Stairway to Heaven," the audience stood up and sang the lyrics in unison, raising the roof of Madison Square Garden.

My friend Jenni Trent, the personal assistant of Ahmet Ertegun, had managed to get me two free tickets, and I invited Peter Kobziar, the singer and guitar player of the Volcanos, to come with me. It was a fantastic event but I was shocked and saddened to learn that, although most of the musicians on stage had had a musical relationship with Giorgio in one way or another, nobody had invited him to attend. It showed me that a deep rift still existed between him and his former colleagues.

Later on that year, when I needed a drummer to play when we were recording some songs by my friend Patrick Kurtkowiak, Giorgio put me in touch with Sami, the drummer of the Volcanos. Naturally, I went to see him play with his band at Trude Heller's, a well-known club in Greenwich Village, where I met the other musicians: two Ukrainian-Americans, one German-American, and Sami the Frenchie. We got along fine and I was later invited to be Sami's witness at his City Hall wedding during the summer of 1982.

As Sami was preparing his return to France, which he did two months after his marriage ceremony, he was replaced on the drums by a third Ukrainian-American. After several meetings, the band asked me to become their manager. I accepted with pleasure, and gave them a strict regime of regular rehearsals at Giorgio's house. This led me to spend even more time at the house at 140 West 24th Street over the next few years.

10. REHEARSING AT GIORGIO'S

with recollections from Roman Iwasiwka

The Volcanos: Roman Iwasiwka (bass guitar, vocals), Sami (drums), Peter Kobziar (guitar, vocals), and Peter Glass (guitar, vocals) at Max's Kansas City on September 15, 1982. Photo courtesy of George Bezushko ©1982

The Volcanos were a band that played in New York clubs and at Ukrainian house parties, and there were regular music events at Giorgio's house too. All kinds of musicians were passing through the house at this time, and others such as the popular S&M club Paddles held its own private parties there on a weekly basis.

When we came to rehearse at night, lovely, young ladies were walking around with ping pong paddles in their hands. Dressed like maids, their uniforms were open at the back, revealing their naked backsides. They walked around, slapping paying customers on the backside and tweaking those who were wearing visible nipple clamps.

The Paddles club team left their sadomasochist props and tools on the ground floor so that they did not have to be brought again for each party. There were large crosses where clients could be tied, big phallic pieces of all kinds, dozens of paddles hanging from the ceiling, etc. This inspired Peter Kobziar, who surely did not need any encouragement to start with, to write more and more songs with erotic lyrics for the Volcanos. I produced several of our music events there when Paddles was closed and our audience seemed to enjoy the unusual decorations without understanding what these "arty pieces" actually were.

I also produced two free concerts, one in Battery Park on August 11, 1984, and one a week later in Tompkins Square Park. Scotty worked the sound desk for these two concerts and Giorgio let us borrow his sound system for free. The music on those two days was pumped out loud and clear and a great time was had by the music-lovers who attended. We were all indebted to Giorgio, without whom none of this could have happened. The city was recovering from an economic recession and a few years later there were serious riots in the park following protests by local people about the gentrification of the park and the treatment of homeless people there. Due to a crack epidemic, crime figures were surging throughout the city and drug use was high.

One night when I was on the door at a Volcanos' gig, two cops came in and told me about a serious incident involving my girlfriend and a friend of hers. They drove me back home in their car and explained that the two women had been assaulted by two armed men in our apartment building. My girlfriend and her friend were on their way to the Volcanos' gig, when they were forced to go back inside the apartment, and raped at gunpoint.

When I arrived, I could hardly recognize the place. Everything was turned upside down. Detectives were checking everything with special lights and they had dusted the place for fingerprints. My stereo system had been stolen, but strangely enough, my Apple IIe computer was still there. The thieves had only stolen a few small items. My girlfriend was sitting there trembling, tears rolling down her cheeks and her friend had already been driven to the hospital. A policeman drove my girlfriend to the hospital soon afterwards, as she had calmed down after my arrival.

The women had been hurt both physically and mentally. Over several days, we had to go to the police station so that they could look at hundreds of photographs of known criminals. My girlfriend was able to identify one individual who turned out to have a long rap sheet. With the help of the police, he was prosecuted and convicted. While many

The Volcanos (*Left to right*) Peter Kobziar, Peter Strutynski, Roman Iwasiwka and Peter Glass in Battery Park, 1984

Scott MacAuley, sound engineer, in Tompkins Square Park, New York , 1984

women fear facing their aggressors in court, she wanted him to be convicted and incarcerated for as long as possible. She asked me not to attend the trial and I did as she asked. The perpetrator received a life sentence.

This experience gave me a new respect for New York cops. I saw the way they dealt with people in distress professionally, how they carried out their search of the apartment and conducted the case in a thorough manner.

The impact of the crime on my girlfriend and our loss of a sense of safety in the neighbourhood took its toll on me emotionally, and I confided in Giorgio. He was always there when I was upset or needed to speak to someone, on the phone or in person. But his financial situation continued to deteriorate seriously, and Paddles was the saving grace that prevented him from drowning, augmented by the meager revenues generated by the few bands that were still rehearsing there and whose numbers were dwindling in the economic downturn.

At least, Paddles was a serious and reliable tenant. They kept the place clean, and they paid their rent on time. To thank us for our help in keeping the house going by rehearsing in the building, Giorgio offered to produce the recording of the songs of the Volcanos for free. But the band had come to a standstill artistically. Musical tastes were changing, the musicians were getting tired, and it felt like the group was about to break up at any moment, after having played together constantly for four years.

Scott MacAuley, who still lived in the house, was roped in as the sound engineer. Everything was recorded live, and Giorgio produced twelve tracks in one night in December 1984. However, in spite of Giorgio's best efforts to help the band, the Volcanos broke up after performing a New Year's Eve concert at the Xenia Motel, out in the Catskills, where many Ukrainian-Americans reside.

Roman Iwasiwka, bass player and singer for the Volcanos, recalled the band rehearsing in Giorgio's house:

"The Volcanos were rehearsing and we went into a rare jam, and I remember going into a bass line that was not unlike the last half of Santana's "Black Magic Woman" when the door opened and Giorgio told us to "keep playing, don't stop." A few minutes later he brought five or six drummers (maybe from Senegal) into the room as they were drumming to the same beat that we were playing. I often think about that moment and wonder if he was up in his apartment when he noticed that the two bands in two different rooms were in synchronicity. And what were the odds of that happening?

I also remember one event where Giorgio introduced a harmonizer machine (I think it was on loan) to the Volcanos to "play with," and we did some recordings. He gave us a toy to play with and I think he was curious to see what we would make of it.

The other memory was when I was assisting Ken Regan to photograph Rod Stewart at Madison Square Garden for an HBO special, and he and I were backstage when we ran into Giorgio. At the time, I think I was a bit skeptical (before the Internet and Wikipedia) of what connections Giorgio really had or what embellishments to stories were made until Rod Stewart passed by and yelled out, "Hey, Giorgio," and Giorgio responded with a happy, "Hey, Rod!" I knew at that very moment that Giorgio was who he was."

Surgery

After the breakup of the Volcanos, three of the musicians got together with Sergei Zholobetsky, a guitarist/singer/composer who had recently immigrated from Ukraine, and they asked me to become their manager.

We were casting around for a name for the new band, so I asked Giorgio for ideas. He suggested the name Lifetime Warranty. When I mentioned this to the musicians, they thought Giorgio must have been joking.

We finally agreed on the name of Surgery, based on Sergei's name – Serge in English. The music would have to cut like a knife.

I proposed we do a music event fundraiser in aid of the restoration of the Statue of Liberty, and since we were all immigrants, or children of immigrants, they accepted.

We spent a lot of time together rehearsing at Giorgio's after work, and then we'd go to Lys Mykyta (Sly Fox), the bar

Roman Iwasiwka
Photo: Peter Iwasiwka ©2016

within the Ukrainian National Home building, located at 140 Second Avenue between St. Marks Place and Ninth Street in the East Village, to talk about our projects.

On December 12, 1985, as I was leaving Lys Mykyta to go home, I heard on the radio at the bar there, that Ian Stewart, the sixth Rolling Stone, who had cofounded the band and was their extraordinary original blues and boogie piano player, had just died of a massive heart attack while he was visiting his doctor. Although I'd never met him, I felt sad, as his music had touched me deeply for years. I called Giorgio to tell him, and the news hit him hard. Stu and Giorgio had worked together organizing the band's marketing and gigs in its early days of 1963.

Our rehearsals paid off and our upcoming fundraiser for the Statue of Liberty was motivating us to work hard so I felt we were ready to record a few tracks. I called Ahmet Ertegun, the cofounder and chairman of Atlantic Records, and explained the nature of our project to his assistant, Jennilynd Trent. Ahmet was an immigrant from Turkey, and Jenni was from Jamaica. Ahmet asked me to come in and

Surgery: (*Left to right*) Andrij Sonevytsky, Sergei Zholobetsky, Roman Iwasiwka, and Peter Strutynski

117

bring along a tape recording of the band, so I recorded one of the rehearsals at Giorgio's, and went along to his office at the Warner Building at 75 Rockefeller Plaza.

Ahmet played the tape right away on his stereo, so loud that I was afraid his windows were going to shatter. He listened for a while, thought for a moment, stopped the tape, and told me that it reminded him of Roxy Music, Brian Ferry's band, which Ahmet had distributed for years. However, he'd recently stopped representing Roxy as he felt their sound was no longer in vogue. Nevertheless, he asked me to come back once the record was finished so that he could pass it along to his A&R department.

We recorded two songs at Planet Studios then shot a video on Liberty Island, the site of the Statue of Liberty, on June 23, 1985, the last day it was open to the public before closing for restoration. We released a single and organized a cruise for a hundred people in New York Harbour on July 26th with a stop by the statue, which was basking gloriously in a superb, fiery sunset.

Next, I produced a concert at Casa Galicia, a private club located under the Ritz hotel. This place was owned by a group of Freemasons, and since it was not much in use, they let us rent it for a small amount. Once again, the gig was jam-packed and we moved ahead with our fundraising, which I named Operation: Face-Lift.

At a friend's house party, I met a young French woman, Natasha, who had an unusual act. Using a black light effect, she would dance and take off her clothes, effectively disappearing, except for her white lingerie and some dayglo makeup on her face and nails. When I mentioned it to Giorgio, he suggested that I invite her to come over and dance at one of the band's rehearsals.

The musicians had no idea of her act when she walked in, so she did her show, and they soon asked her to perform with them at the next concert at the Bitter End on December 11, 1985. Everything seemed to be going well but Giorgio was losing interest in the band. Although he liked Roman's personality and voice, he did not like Serge, whose personality, voice, and military haircut grated on him. When the band broke up in July 1986, Giorgio was not surprised.

Nine years later, we were shocked to discover that Serge had been arrested by Interpol in a Greek monastery, of all places. He had gone back to Kyiv, where he had bought a hotel from the proceeds of a scam involving defrauding Medicare for 11 million dollars. The whole sorry story was told in an article in the *Times Herald-Record* of Middletown published on December 12, 1996.

Who could have predicted this when I was drinking vodka with Serge ten years earlier in Giorgio's house, while toasting the success of our fundraiser for the Statue of Liberty?

When I told Giorgio the story, he just looked me in the eye and asked, "How come you did not see it coming?"

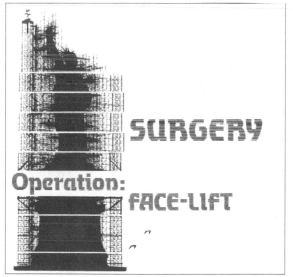

Front cover of the single for "Operation Face-Lift" 1985

The French Doric Room in the building of the Grand Lodge of New York where L'Union Française Nº17 holds its meetings

11. FRIENDSHIP AND BROTHERHOOD

"I was always for the underdog, anyway."- GOMELSKY

Giorgio and I liked to hang out together and he became like an older brother to me. In spite of our differences, we had a lot in common: our mothers were both called Eliane, we had both lived in Mediterranean countries when we were young, we had both learned to play blues music on the church organs near to our high schools, and we grew up listening to jazz and blues music on foreign radio stations at night.

When we moved to New York City, we were both unattached, footloose and fancy-free, living on a shoestring and devoted to music. Our futures were uncertain, like an open book, and perhaps craving to belong to a community of some sort, we were both attracted to become active members and officers of an old and venerable Masonic Lodge.

On December 2, 1986, Giorgio invited me to go with him to see a jazz concert by the Charlie Watts Orchestra at the Ritz. We drank a little too much – whisky for him, and beer for me – but the concert was really great. Even though everybody had come to see him perform as the famous drummer of the Rolling Stones, Charlie stuck to the jazz numbers that he had always loved, playing with an excellent group of bona fide jazz musicians.

When one of the musicians got absorbed in a solo that became a little too convoluted, Giorgio told me that the guy was "noodling," and he explained the meaning of the expression and how the musician was lost in his own weave.

At the end of the concert, we went backstage and Giorgio introduced me to Charlie. I was in awe to be shaking the hand of the iconic drummer of the Rolling Stones.

Tony King, the Stones' publicist came over and gently took Giorgio's arm to usher us out to make room for other friends and fans who wanted to talk to Charlie. On his way out, Giorgio gave Charlie the address of the Tramps nightclub, which was located close to the Ritz, and where Giorgio worked as a DJ introducing audiences to world music. He asked Charlie to pass by and say hello. We sat at Tramps and waited, a stretch limo passed by, Charlie's face appeared at the window, then the limo sped up, and Charlie disappeared into the night. Giorgio was bitterly disappointed but Charlie was never really much of a socialite.

We walked back to his house where Bullit, a talented but broke musician, who often slept on the floor of the second floor rehearsal studio, was sitting with a group of friends. They were improvising their own brand of world music on the ground floor, and that was exactly the medicine Giorgio needed to feel better.

Giorgio switched on the PA system, I took a blues harp out of my pocket, Giorgio grabbed a bongo, and we lost ourselves in an endless blues where each of us could express his own frustrations about life in a "mean old world."

He lived alone, although there were always women who were attracted by his energy and magnetism. He was never happy in his amorous relationships, perhaps because women tried to make him more domesticated, more monogamous, like trying to tame a tiger. We spent a lot of time on the phone exchanging our views on the feminine psyche.

I loved his spontaneity. Sometimes, he would call me at midnight to ask me to go to a party with him. His fame

Charlie Watts playing jazz in Switzerland, 2010. Photo: Poiseon

meant that he would immediately be surrounded by all kinds of people as soon as we arrived, and of course I benefited from the aura that surrounded him too. He thought that I would be a wonderful father, and that I should have children. "Women have the gardens, men have the seeds, don't let yours be thrown away in the winds of carelessness." There was a kind of Russian mysticism about him and his old-fashioned sayings would often make me stop and wonder for a while, even though he had fathered three children from three women in three different countries.

During one of these conversations, an attractive young woman walked into his apartment to undertake some building work. She did not look like a construction worker, but she was carrying a heavy window frame with ease and was clearly working away with skill and strength. The next day, Giorgio told me that she liked me, and that she wanted to invite me to her place. It was a first for me and perhaps it demonstrated the growing confidence of young women in the 80s. I was flattered, but I was also a little daunted by her.

While the band rehearsed in the studio, I would often sit in the corridor and read books. One night, Giorgio passed by and asked me what kind of book I was reading. It was about esoteric philosophies, and Giorgio was interested to know more. He knew that I regularly attended the meetings of a French-speaking Masonic lodge, L'Union Française No. 17, which was instituted on December 26, 1797, and which was therefore the oldest French association in continuous existence in the United States. Its headquarters were located in the building of the Grand Lodge of the State of New York at 71 West 23rd Street – which was literally 500 feet from Giorgio's house.

I first joined the lodge in 1983 and had become an officer by that time. This opened up many conversations with Giorgio, who turned out to be erudite in many fields such as Greek tragedy and Elizabethan theatre. Of course he knew all about French writers, as well as individuals who had left their mark on Russian culture, from Grigori Rasputin to Sergei Diaghilev. He even adopted the name of Oscar Rasputin as his nom de plume to take composer's credit for the Yardbirds' instrumental "Got to Hurry," played by a very young Eric Clapton. The name of Rasputin did actually fit him like a glove.

Eventually, Giorgio asked me to sponsor him and introduce him to our lodge, and I accepted with pleasure and told him that I regarded it as a great privilege. I read him the presentation, and then asked him, "What is the main reason that has motivated you to want to join?" He gave me a peaceful look and replied, "Because I am tired of searching alone."

This was the most beautiful and honest answer I had ever heard. I was surprised, however, to hear this man, who had always been surrounded by famous and talented artists, tell me that, deep down inside, his heady lifestyle was not enough to truly satisfy him. He was searching for another way to build his own spiritual temple.

I gave him a warm smile and found in his eyes the peaceful, direct, and frank assurance of a man who was happy to have made the choice to get involved with something he had been looking for.

On April 15, 1986, Giorgio was initiated at L'Union Française No. 17, where his dynamism became contagious. He was a true breath of fresh air who walked into our old institution, and he immediately offered us his talent as a great communicator by putting at our disposal his professional video camera at a time when most people could not have access to this technology, since we were still in the analog world of 1986.

L'Union Française was about to celebrate its 190th anniversary, and Giorgio offered to produce and direct a documentary on its history and its current members. We set up an interview with Léon H. Depas, who not only knew the history of our lodge better than anyone but he had also gathered a large collection of historical documents.

Léon's house in Queens was also the office of his accounting firm, and there was plenty of space to build a production studio for the day's shoot. Léon's family came from Haiti, and they were all extremely kind and generous individuals who gave us the greatest hospitality possible. Giorgio was in heaven. Everybody respected him for his technical prowess, but at the same time, he felt the sincere warmth emanating from them to him. We were very far away from the music business.

Actually, this was just the continuation of his previous experience with us. The first time I took him to the bar in the basement of our headquarters, Giorgio had told me how much he had appreciated the courteous and friendly exchanges that he had observed when I introduced him to members of Italian, Hispanic, Greek, and American lodges.

We spent three nights in one of the editing rooms at Antenne 2, which Nicole Devilaine kindly let us use, and the documentary was finally ready, just in time to be shown to our guests during the special evening we had organized for our 190th anniversary on October 20, 1987.

Everybody appreciated the film although some were rather surprised that we had access to such expensive video equipment, which was not commonplace at the time.

We decided to open our lodge to the public on a Sunday afternoon and organized a get-together in a French restaurant located near Columbus Circle. We invited guest speakers who could talk on various matters of public interest for French expats, such as Professeur Maman, senator of the French residents of our electoral district who answered questions regarding the recent changes in the French social security system. Long-term expats were not aware of all the recent changes, and ramifications that could affect their retirement plans, and it was not always easy for them to find the right answers to their questions.

Giorgio generously offered us access to his computers to create and print attractive invitations, at a time when most people had no idea what a personal computer could be used for. He was soon in his element again. The Masonic Lodge provided a new outlet for his creative energies. One suggestion he made was to start recording a series of video interviews with the members of L'Union Française, starting with the oldest ones. This was to be a complete modernization of our archives. We started with Joseph Hemous, a former French police officer who had served in Africa, in countries which were former French colonies, and who was now working at the French Mission of the United Nations. Giorgio operated the camera and I conducted the interview.

When we were done, we left the tape on a shelf and made plans to edit it later at Antenne 2, in the hope that Nicole would let us use her editing suite again. However, when I went to Giorgio's house a few days later, he told me that he was really sorry but one of his musicians had to do a video recording for his band, and had erased our interview so that he could tape his own material. My heart sank, and I realized that we would need to find a way to protect the tapes from re-use, and that I would have to start all over again.

In 1991, I loaned Giorgio some money at L'Union Française, and he paid me back later by cheque. He was very proud to have finally been able to open a cheque account, and this was only the fourth cheque he had ever written on that account. Of course, being a collector of memorabilia, I never deposited his cheque so that I could keep his autograph in my archives.

Giorgio Gomelsky's signed cheque on April 16, 1991

Apart from the few freelance jobs I managed to get at Antenne 2 when Nicole had special projects she could swing my way, I sold French wine in order to pay the rent, and as I never cooked, I had nothing but champagne in my fridge – champagne which I bought from a colleague who worked for another wine company, and who sold me dirt cheap cases of his samples.

I was subletting a room with a bathroom in a large apartment at the corner of Central Park South and Broadway, where I slept on a mattress on the floor. The single redeeming feature of the apartment was that my view of Central Park and Columbus Circle was unbeatable. When Giorgio came to see me, we'd take a bottle of champagne from the fridge, with an ice bucket, a couple of glasses, and go up to the terrace on the twenty-first floor, with Central Park at our feet. We'd sit there watching the ballet of airplanes dancing in the northeast corner of the sky as they flew in and out of La Guardia airport, talking freely about everything that came to mind.

Whenever I visited Giorgio at his place, we'd sit up in the loft space that Ronnie Bird had built for him on the top floor. Giorgio would lovingly prepare tasty soups in the small kitchen and we would savour eating them, while sampling the various French wines that I used to bring with me from the Bordeaux wine company where I worked.

Somehow we both survived on a shoestring. He used to repair everything in the house himself, from the water heater to the bathtub, which he had built himself and of which he was very proud. Sometimes, problems were a bit more difficult to solve, as when the next door neighbour complained about the noise coming from the PA system, and the cops or firemen would come to "inspect" what was going on, knowing pretty well where to find the cash that Giorgio always "forgot" in the basement.

Necessity being the mother of invention, one day Giorgio came up with a plan to make some money fast. The building at the corner of 24th Street and 7th Avenue had been demolished. New foundations were being dug in the granite and mounds of broken stones were sitting there waiting for trucks to take them away early in the morning.

Giorgio's big idea was to take some of these stones surreptitiously during the night, break them up into tiny pieces and then insert a fragment of stone into a transparent plastic cube, which we would market as a novelty labelled "a piece of Manhattan," to tourists. The idea was original, but of course, I knew who would be expected to sell these novelties in the street, and it was not going to be Giorgio. I didn't take him up on it. I always avoided forming a business partnership with Giorgio, as it would, inevitably, have ruined our friendship.

The mood in the country was changing as the recession hit ordinary people. The constant round of parties began to pall, and we'd often talk late into the night on the phone lamenting the state of our love lives, as girlfriends tended to come and go.

Giorgio began to fall out of love with the world too as his constant money problems dragged him down. He was spending more and more time alone at home, becoming morose. His tendency to drown his sorrows with drink or drugs was not helping. His old friends came to visit less and less often. The city was reeling from the effects of Reagonomics, with homelessness on the rise and benefits for the poorest being cut. As an illegal immigrant, Giorgio must have been worried that if he lost the house, he might be forced to leave the country. Moreover, Giorgio was in his fifties, and was well aware that his youthful adventures were far behind him.

"I hated the music business, I hated the film business, I hated anything to do with any business that dealt with art. To me, it was a bad business. They were not doing it right. And I was pushing for the artists to create their own business: You remain the owner of your work, and you share the profits thereof. Like this, you will keep the thing authentic."– GOMELSKY

Commodore Amiga 1000 personal computer with 1081
RGB monitor, 1985. Photo: Kaiiv/Pixel8

12.DOUBLE REBIRTH

In 1986, Giorgio was clearly suffering from a bout of depression that confined him to bed a lot of the time. Although I still went two or three times a week to his studio for the band's rehearsals, which were held on the second floor right below his bedroom, I rarely caught sight of him. First a cat moved into the property and made it her home, catching the mice that scurried around the building, and then around this time Giorgio adopted a wonderful dog, a brown and white pointer. It was not surprising that the dog helped him to recover, mainly due to the exercise of taking him on daily walks and caring for another sentient being. He called the dog Irzu, and when I saw them out and about in the neighbourhood, Giorgio looked happy to be out walking or riding his bicycle with Irzu by his side.

Giorgio regained the energy to make a fresh start. "To hell with the music industry," he said. His ability to see the coming trends enabled him to see another kind of future which was emerging due to the availability of personal computers and the internet. Since I owned an Apple IIe, I understood his passion for the Amiga computers that were distributed by Commodore. These computers were completely different from those of Apple, IBM, Sony, etc. because they worked with an operating system which allowed users to exchange their own programs and to create new ones freely.

This new, free and democratic tool was like a dream come true for him. He had always preferred non-conformity to the legal restrictions and issues around copyright that exist for the owners of commercial products in the businesses of music, software, computers, and the internet. He immediately understood the possibilities of the technology and the radical ideas of the internet gurus who wanted to make knowledge freely available to all for the benefit of humanity.

For Giorgio, this new means of worldwide communication was as important as Gutenberg's invention of the printing press. He could see that the internet would enable free international exchanges and bring in a means of production and transmission in real time that would allow people to escape censorship and regulation.

Since nobody had an email address or even simple access to the internet at that time, Giorgio put together a group of fans of the Amiga computers, the Amigans, who met regularly at his place to share information and trade the software programs they were developing.

When Amiga created an American national competition so that fans could submit their own projects, Giorgio won first prize two or three years in a row with his own digital avant-garde video creations, which he produced with the Video Toaster, an inexpensive software program for video editing that easily rivalled the extremely expensive editing suites used by the best professional video studios.

Thanks to his performance in these annual competitions, Giorgio won additional software programs, which permitted him to become even more creative with his own videos.

He built a huge U-shaped console table on which he set a dozen computers linked to each other. It looked like something from the Starship Enterprise of the *Star Trek* series, and Giorgio had become his own version of Captain Kirk. "Beam me up, Scotty."

He produced a cable television program that he called *esc=shift=cntrl,* in which he presented his own oral history of rock and roll music, and advanced new ideas for the creation and development of a netcast network that he wanted to launch.

Giorgio had rediscovered his spirit of creativity and was full of energy again, but he was still in deep financial crisis. Somehow he managed to carry on, but nobody could understand how he was doing it.

Another veil was lifted at the end of 1986. Giorgio had been living as an illegal alien in the United States for several years, but on November 6th, during the presidency of Ronald Reagan, an act of Congress gave a chance for illegal immigrants like him to benefit from an amnesty program. Giorgio had to find a lawyer fast, but he lacked the funds to pay for the paperwork necessary to do so and to secure a permanent resident visa.

Etienne Merle, a member of L'Union Française, and I offered to cover the costs, and after several months of legal wrangling, Giorgio came out of the shadows. He was finally allowed to travel abroad and visit his children in Europe without any fear of being caught at the border by immigration officers on the way back, and of being deported for life from the United States. It was a huge relief for him, and Giorgio was very grateful for our help.

For my 40th birthday, I organized a party at Giorgio's. About a hundred and fifty people attended and they were quite surprised to find themselves in the midst of an S&M club. Many did not understand what the tools that hung on the walls were for, and some actually believed that they were in an art gallery. A huge bouquet of beautiful flowers sent from Ithaca by Etienne Merle stood on the bar that Giorgio had set by the entrance door.

I invited people from all walks of life, and the range

of professions and ethnicities was amazing: musicians, businessmen, producers, restaurant owners, wine salesmen, drivers, and a group of Freemasons.

I left at 3 a.m. with a female friend who wanted to give me a special birthday treat, and I returned to Giorgio's at sunrise to gather my gifts and the leftover cases of beer. Where else could I have enjoyed a better 40th birthday party than in the house of Giorgio Gomelsky?

Now that this rite of passage was done with, the question I asked myself daily was: "What was I going to do with the rest of my life?"

I had been surviving with odd jobs at Antenne 2 in New York. I slept on a mattress on the floor in an apartment I was renting on a monthly basis with no long-term contract, and I was not building anything for my future. If I did not find a solution soon, I would forever be carrying the equipment of French journalists at Antenne 2 for peanuts, and only ever be a whisker away from personal bankruptcy.

Meanwhile, I saw that Giorgio had come out of the midlife crisis that had caused him to feel depressed for a long time, and that he was doing better than ever. On the one hand, he had managed to save and keep the house; on the other, he had thrown himself whole-heartedly into this new passion that he shared with his group of Amigans. Consequently, he seemed very happy to have found a new mission and a new tribe.

One evening, I found myself in the bathroom of a seedy bar, and I caught sight of myself in the mirror. I did not look good, and I knew that I had to find a way to change my life. There had to be something I could do to reinvent myself and build a stable future. But I did not know what that something was, or how I was supposed to get there.

When I woke up in the morning, the solution dawned on me loud and clear: I was going to become an actor. Not a stage actor, as I could never make a living with my French accent on the New York stage, but a screen actor who could find work in television and radio commercials as well as in movies and television programs.

I had already felt this calling years earlier when I had been forced to close my independent cable television studio in 1980, but I'd never had the courage to go after my dream of becoming an actor then.

But this time, maybe because my back really was against the wall, I promised myself that I was actually going to go for it body and soul. When I shared this idea with my so-called friends, the feedback was unanimous: "Who do you think you are?"; "What did you smoke today?" Not one single word of support.

One night when Giorgio and I were sitting on the terrace of my building, quietly sipping champagne with Central Park at our feet, I mentioned the idea of becoming an actor and my need for reinvention.

Giorgio suddenly sat up and stared deep into my eyes without uttering a word. I was afraid that I had exposed myself too much, and that I was about to be ridiculed, but after a long pause, he told me to run with it because, if I did not try, I would never know if I could have succeeded.

I breathed a deep sigh of relief and sensed the importance of this intimate moment between us. He was encouraging me to dare to become the person I wanted to be, as he had done with so many people before me. I was sitting there with a man who was not afraid of rejection or failure. A master of reinvention, he knew how to deal with misfortune, how to recover from loss, how to bounce back – just as he had done with the Yardbirds after the Rolling Stones dropped him in London, and then again in Paris after the demise of Paragon, and then in New York after various disappointments in Paris.

When I told him about the reactions I'd had from other people, his answer reminded me of my grandmother's words when I was little: "It's only those who do nothing who never make mistakes."

Giorgio also told me to listen to my own internal tuning fork and to ignore other people's negative comments, particularly those who had never done anything to get out of their daily rut, and to be even more wary of the opinions of my own relatives and inner circle, because these people would always want to see me as they already knew me, and therefore they would never accept my desire to evolve in a different sphere from their own.

He also recalled that many people had advice to give him about the production of music, even though they had never produced anything themselves. He would always say, "First you produce your own record, and then we'll talk."

He concluded by telling me that I should find out right away what I had to do to join the actors' unions, principally the Screen Actors Guild, or SAG, and to move in this new direction as fast as possible without ever looking back.

This was the biggest encouragement anybody had ever given me: "Trust your instincts totally and don't let anybody distract you with their worthless opinions since, in all likelihood, they do not know what they are talking about." At that moment, I realized that Giorgio had just helped me open a new chapter in my life.

He sat back in his armchair, his cigarillo in his left hand and his empty flute of champagne in his right. I stood up, asked him to wait patiently for my return, and went downstairs to pick up another bottle of champagne, excited at the prospect of reinventing myself anew.

My research into joining the acting profession went well. When I had some free time in the office of Antenne 2, I checked the lists of agents, producers, directors, and casting directors that I had purchased in specialty stores. I read the trade magazine *Backstage*, where casting notices were posted. I recorded voice tracks for Antenne 2 when we needed to overdub news stories that we received in English from CBS – recordings that were made by Ronnie Bird, and I kept those for my own demos. I answered questions on camera that were recorded by Francis Freedland for the 8 p.m. evening news broadcast in France in an interview that helped me boost my self-esteem, thanks to Freedland's telling me that I looked good on camera. And Giorgio regularly asked me about my progress, just like an older brother checking on a sibling.

In July of 1987, I asked Roman Iwasiwka, who was not just a musician but also the photo assistant to the great photographer Ken Regan at Camera 5, to take some publicity shots of me to use as my official portraits to send to agents. I showed them to Giorgio and asked him to help me select one.

Slowly, I began to put myself out there. I first found non-union background work. Next, I was booked for a small part for an industrial film that was shot in Cincinnati, in which I played a French businessman. This was the job that qualified me to join SAG, a key step in my professional life, that helped me to launch myself in my new career.

During the spring of 1988, I decided to produce a kind of musical TV talent show in which three bands would compete for cash prizes. The technical crew of Antenne 2 agreed to shoot the video professionally with four high resolution video cameras, my friend Jenni of Atlantic Records helped me find the bands, and Scotty, Giorgio's sound engineer, who had always helped me with the Volcanos and Surgery, found the audio recording equipment we needed and agreed to be the sound engineer for the project.

I booked Studio 54, which the owner, Mark Fleischman,

had inherited from Steve Rubell, and Mark rented it to me on June 12, 1988. I called Art Collins, who had left the Stones' office to become Joe Jackson's manager. He came to my place and, as we talked about the project, he suggested a great name for the show: *Rock Search* – which was perfect.

I still needed a panel, and reached out to Giorgio. He came onboard with his friends Bob Gruen (John Lennon's photographer in New York) and Valerie Warner (a public relations specialist in the world of show business), Rob Fraboni (the producer and engineer for Bob Dylan and the Band, Eric Clapton, Keith Richards, the Beach Boys, and for the concert film *The Last Waltz,* directed by Martin Scorcese), and Alvenia Bridges (a public relations specialist who had worked with the Rolling Stones).

Scotty composed a rock theme for the show. He played and recorded all the instruments at Giorgio's, and Chichi (a friend of Jenni's) gave me digital designs that we edited as a backdrop for the titles of the show. Finally, Scotty got permission to edit the program in an editing suite that was being used by the Talking Heads during the day, but that was free at night. Scotty wanted to edit it himself to show that he was able to do it, have his own demo reel to prove it, and maybe look for work in editing later on. After several nights of intense editing, we had a great program. None of it could have happened without Giorgio's help and support, without the equipment he lent me, and without the many people he brought onboard, including Scotty.

The house was once again full of life and excitement. A lot of people were coming and going, including musicians he knew from France, actors, and of course, hangers on.

On January 29, 1989, Giorgio produced a benefit concert at the Kitchen Club for the lyricist Egon Bondy of the Czech band Plastic People of the Universe. The sax player in exile Vratislav Brabenec was invited to join New York musicians like Ed Pastorini, the Soldier String Quartet, Craig Harris, Borbetomagus, Elliott Sharp, and Gary Lucas, and they performed together a large part of the Plastic People of the Universe's songbook.

This event, which Giorgio created and produced, gave positive support to people in Prague where the countercultural movement that had gathered around the Plastics in the 1970s would finally lead to the Velvet Revolution in November of that year, led by playwright Vaclav Havel.

A month before that, on October 28, 1989, the Rolling Stones gave a concert at Shea Stadium in support of *Steel Wheels*, their comeback album after a five-year break up. Shea Stadium was the home of the Mets, a baseball team in Queens, that was large enough for an audience of 55,000 people. The first band to ever play a music concert at Shea had been the Beatles on August 15, 1965, and they had played there again on Tuesday, August 23, 1966, just six days before their very last concert at San Francisco's Candlestick Park on August 29, 1966.

Giorgio managed to get us tickets to see the Stones, and we took the No. 7 train to Shea Stadium. The fan in me was elated to go see the Stones in the company of their first 'de facto' manager. However, Giorgio was upset because he had

reached out to Bill Wyman for backstage passes so we could go and say 'hi' to the band after their concert, but to no avail.

The panel of *Rock Search* at Studio 54 (*L to r*) Rob Fraboni, Valerie Warner, Bob Gruen, Alvenia Bridges and Giorgio

During the summer of that year, I met Joan Osborne, who was a singer at a private party for Atlantic Records. Joan was an extraordinary young blues singer from Kentucky, and I spoke to her after her performance. We got along well.

I told her that I'd be happy to help her develop her career, and she agreed to discuss it further. I decided to produce a live recording of one of her concerts at Mondo Cane, a blues club in Greenwich Village, and we signed a basic agreement. On December 9, 1989, I went to the club with Scotty, and we brought some recording equipment, borrowed once again from Giorgio. Scotty set up the mikes and equipment in the club before the concert, and the band played to a full house. The concert was hot, and Joan gave it her best.

Scotty and I sat in the service staircase to control the levels of the 4-track reel-to-reel tape recorder, and we recorded her two sets. We packed up and returned to Giorgio's house, where we spent the night mixing the best version of each song. The master was ready by daybreak.

As the Berlin Wall had just fallen, Giorgio suggested that Joan should go to Europe with her band and play the local clubs in France and Germany, ending with a video to be shot at the remnants of the Berlin Wall. But when we suggested the idea to Joan, she reacted as if Giorgio and I were from another planet, and she turned the idea down flat.

However, once again, Giorgio's instincts for a way to get great publicity proved to be correct, because a few months later that's exactly what Roger Waters ended up doing when he produced a concert of Pink Floyd's album *The Wall* in the 'no man's land' by the remnants of the Berlin Wall on July 21, 1990.

DOUBLE REBIRTH

"The technology, you can't stop it. I saw it go from being
mono to being twice forty-eighty tracks, to Phil Collins'
pre-recorded effects, and God knows what ...
Fair enough, but don't confuse that with art."
– GOMELSKY

The Wall - Live in Berlin was performed on July 21st, 1990, by Roger
Waters and guests near the Potsdamer Platz, Berlin, to commemorate
the fall of the wall. The concert was broadcast internationally.
Photo: German Federal Archives

"We missed out in America big time because we had a
ten-record deal with A&M – 6,000 dollars in advance per
record – but they did not like what we were doing.
Jerry Moss hated it." – GOMELSKY

Giorgio at the wedding reception of Francis and Lilian Dumaurier
on September 29, 1991

13. LOOKING BACK, LOOKING AHEAD

Not long after I joined SAG and started my new acting career, my life was turned upside down because I met my future wife, Lilian.

My relationship with Joan Osborne had fallen apart because she decided to go in the direction of pop music rather than stay with the blues. She signed with a big label and later had a hit with the single "One of Us." This experience put me off the music industry entirely and I decided to bow out of the business for a while.

On April 21, 1991, Giorgio told me the news that his friend Steve Marriott had died the night before in a fire that had engulfed his 16th century home while he was sleeping. It was probable that the fire had been started by a cigarette which had been left burning in his bedroom. Steve was only 44 years old, and Giorgio was really upset by the news.

However, my new relationship had changed our friendship as I was spending more time with my new girlfriend than with him. Lilian and I moved in together fairly quickly, and my search for acting work had become a daily obsession too. Although Giorgio and I were still friends, there was no longer the same camaraderie of two single guys hanging out that we had shared for years. Of course, we invited Giorgio, Ronnie, and Jenni to our wedding reception later that year. Giorgio soon struck up a relationship with a woman named

Dawn, a designer. Instead of going out as mates, Giorgio would come to visit us with Dawn, and we'd go out together as couples. Lilian organized several parties in our apartment during 1992, and Giorgio used to come with Dawn to meet friends that we had from other circles. In particular, Lilian had friends from the former Soviet Union and Giorgio had a natural affinity with them, being a refugee himself from the USSR.

Dawn designed clothes, which she enhanced with melted wax appliquéd to the material in vivid colors, and we each had one of her gorgeous decorated waistcoats. Dawn soon became friends with Lilian, and they used to go out together with other female friends. We also went to get-togethers in large apartments on the Upper West Side where Giorgio had friends from his group of Amigans. Dawn also used

Dawn sporting one of her designs at Francis and Lilian's apartment, 1993

to help us decorate the reception hall of L'Union Française when we had social gatherings there.

By 1993, Giorgio had become a main officer of our lodge, and we often met at his place to prepare our ceremonies under Irzu's watchful eye. But his idea of what we should be doing didn't really conform to the rules, and that was not to the liking of other lodge members. In particular, Giorgio would have liked us to become involved in the way New York City was developing. This concept was more European than American, but it was against the rules which specifically prevented lodges from being active in any political and/or religious activities, even though members were encouraged to get involved in such matters outside the lodge, especially if it involved organized charity work.

Unable to change the direction of the lodge, Giorgio stopped coming to the meetings in 1994, even though he retained his membership until 1999. He carried on seeing several of his favourite members long after that, especially those who had helped him through his midlife crisis.

1993 was an important anniversary for the Yardbirds too and Giorgio managed to get Charly Records to release a 4 CD box set with all the recordings he had produced for them, including the recording of the concert with Sonny Boy Williamson, which had become extremely hard to find, even in bootleg form.

The title was simple: *Train Kept a-Rollin': The Complete Giorgio Gomelsky Productions*. It featured different versions of known hits which showed how the band worked progressively to achieve the desired result, as well as all the live recordings that Giorgio had produced with the band, a grand total of ninety tracks.

Giorgio came over to our place to give me my own personal copy from the few he had just received from England. I was very touched that he thought of me for this.

I opened the wrapping and the box. On top of the four CDs, there was a thick booklet of photos, souvenirs, and comments, as well as a grey T-shirt (above) and a badge with the logo of the Yardbirds. I asked Giorgio to autograph the box for me, and he obliged kindly with the special silver marker that he had brought for the occasion.

Lilian asked me to open a bottle of champagne, we played the first CD, and Giorgio was beaming. His baby was finally here, a labour of love that had taken several years to produce, even if it had been released in a limited quantity.

I knew straight away that this box set would become one of my most precious belongings, like my tickets and program for the Woodstock Festival where I spent my first weekend in America in August 1969.

On January 15, 1994, Giorgio invited a few friends over to his place for a private party. He had recently been given one of the large video screens that had been used during the U2 Zoo TV Tour, and it was obviously a good excuse for having a party. He was at peace with himself and happy to share the moment with us.

To celebrate Giorgio's 60th birthday on February 28, 1994, Nicole Devilaine organized a large party at Chez Joséphine, the French bistro run by Jean-Claude Baker located at 414 West 42nd Street. Jean-Claude was one of the children that Josephine Baker had looked after while she lived in Paris, and I had known him fairly well in 1979 and 1980, when we were both independent cable television producers, and when he left his mark on Manhattan with TeleFrance USA. Nicole had known him since he moved to New York, and she had helped him obtain programs from the old ORTF (the government controlled French Radio and Television Broadcasting Office, which ceased operations on December 31, 1974), such as episodes of the popular Madame Le Juge series with Simone Signoret.

Dawn interviewed me and several of Giorgio's friends and asked them the same three questions: "What do you like about Giorgio?," "What do you dislike about Giorgio?," and "What do you think Giorgio should do with the rest of his life?" The answers were varied, and Dawn screened her video before a small invited audience that evening before going to the restaurant.

I did my best to answer these simple questions diplomatically. The third question was the one I answered best: I thought Giorgio should produce an autobiographical rock opera to show on the ground floor of his house with narration, songs, and slide shows on a screen, things that Giorgio already did at his private parties. He liked the idea and took me by surprise when he told me that, now that he had turned 60, he wanted to start working on his "legacy" anyway. He wanted to organize his mementos, recordings, short films and all the documentation that he had collected in London, Paris, and New York.

He invited me to his place to show me some memorabilia

MICK JAGGER FORMS GROUP

MICK Jagger, R&B voc-, alist, is taking a rhythm and blues group into the Marquee tomorrow night (Thurs) while Blues Inc. is doing its Jazz Club gig.

Called 'The Rolling Stones' ("I hope they don't think we're a rock 'n' roll outfit", says Mick) the lineup is: Jagger, (voc), Keith Richards, Elmo Lewis (gtrs), Dick Taylor (bass), 'Stu' (pno), Mike Avery (drs).

A second group under Long John Baldry will also be there.

that he had kept for years. Since he was only at the beginning of this huge project, he pulled out an envelope with newspaper clippings from 1962 and 1963. The paper had turned yellow and was a little wrinkled, but the text was clear and easy to read. The first clipping was promoting the first show by the Rolling Stones at the Marquee Club in London. Mick Jagger commented that he sang in a rhythm and blues group and declared: "I hope they don't think we're a rock 'n' roll outfit." The band, as listed, featured Mick Jagger on vocals, Keith Richards and Elmo Lewis on guitars, Dick Taylor on bass guitar, Stu on piano, and Mike Avery on drums.

Unfortunately, this clipping was not dated, but it was most probably published shortly before July 12, 1962, when this concert was produced at the Marquee. There were several interesting details to note. Elmo Lewis was the stage name of Brian Jones. Dick Taylor left the band to start the Pretty Things on lead guitar, with Phil May on vocals, and these two artists were still performing, writing, and recording songs as the Pretty Things until Phil May's death on May 15, 2020. Finally, Mick Avory, whose name was misspelled in the clipping, left the band to become the Kinks' drummer.

This clipping also contradicted Mick Avory, who said later (as mentioned in Wikipedia) that he only rehearsed twice with the Rolling Stones at the Bricklayers Arms in Soho but that he did not play with them at the Marquee.

However, a copy of one of the letters handwritten by Brian Jones on July 2, 1962, that he mailed to VIPs of the London blues scene, and that is circulating freely on the internet now, validates Mick Avory's recollection as Brian indicates that the drummer for the event was going to be Earl Phillips.

But an important question remains: who was Earl Phillips? It is highly doubtful that this would have been the same Earl Phillips who played drums with Muddy Waters, Howling Wolf, Jimmy Reed, John Lee Hooker, Snooky Prior, and many others, and this is probably just wishful thinking (with a wink and a nod) on the part of Brian Jones who was going then by the professional name of Elmo Lewis, as seen in the clipping, in homage to Elmore James, Lewis being his actual first name – Brian being, at the time, the only guitar player in England who could really play slide guitar in the style of Elmore James.

When his autobiography *Stone Alone* was published in 1990, Bill Wyman said that Tony Chapman, had played several gigs with this early version of the Rolling Stones during the summer and fall of 1962, and it has been assumed that Tony played also with them during this historic first concert at the Marquee, but Tony himself has said that he did not remember playing with them that day. So the mystery of the true identity of Earl Phillips still remains.

Tony Chapman was also the drummer of The Cliftons, in which Bill Wyman played bass, and it was Tony who recommended Bill as a replacement for Dick Taylor when Dick decided to ditch the bass guitar and become the lead guitar for The Pretty Things, the new band that he formed with Phil May. This is how Bill Wyman showed up at a pub in Chelsea on December 7, 1962 to audition for the band.

The clipping ended with an announcement that Long John Baldry was also going to be part of the show. Long John Baldry was the singer with Alexis Korner's Blues Incorporated with whom he recorded "R&B from the Marquee", and it is important to note that, at various times, Brian Jones, Mick Jagger, Keith Richards, and Charlie Watts also played in Blues Inc. Later on, Long John Baldry would join forces with Rod Stewart, Brian Auger, and Julie Driscoll in Steampacket, a band managed by Giorgio Gomelsky who also produced a couple of live recordings that were never officially released.

This clipping was important for Giorgio for many reasons. He had been the creator and impresario of these new Thursday nights at the Marquee, and Long John Baldry, who was the best-known of them all, provided the much needed support with his musicians. This is when Giorgio really got to know Brian Jones who was the leader of the Rollin' Stones along with Ian Stewart.

In a letter he wrote to a fan named Doreen Pettifer, Brian

Jones explained how the band was formed:

> "The band is really an amalgamation of two bands. The one being an R&B band I formed about a year ago, and the other being a group run by Mick and Keith in S.E. London. I was introduced to Keith and we decided to pool our resources, so with Stu from my band, and Mick from Keith's we became the nucleus of the 'Stones.'
>
> Personnel:
>
> Keith Richards – Guitar – 19 years old – went to Art School, then straight into rhythm and blues.
>
> Mick Jagger – Vocals, Harmonica, 19 years old. London School of Economics.
>
> Charlie Watts – 21, worked in advertising for some years – now full-time musician. (Drummer)
>
> Ian Stewart – Piano, 23, works with I.C.I. as a Shipping Clerk during the day (known affectionately as "Stu")
>
> Bill Wyman – Bass – 23, works during the day as a storekeeper or something equally horrible. Only member of the band married – only one who'll ever be married. Proud father of a baby son (or daughter)
>
> Myself, Brian Jones – Guitar and Harmonica, 21, was studying Architecture – more artistic satisfaction from R & B.
>
> (Mick, Keith, and myself as I expect you noticed, wear our hair out long, the others being more conventional)"

In spite of Brian begging him to book the band for a gig, Giorgio was not impressed enough by the Rollin' Stones to invite them to play as his first house band for the club he was organizing and promoting at the Station Hotel in Richmond in January 1963. Bill Wyman had only joined the band on

December 7, 1962, and Charlie Watts became their drummer in January 1963.

The first band was indeed the Dave Hunt's R&B Band, as is illustrated in the newspaper clipping (above), and Giorgio only invited the Rollin' Stones to play at the Station Hotel on February 24, 1963, after the Dave Hunt's Band got snowed in and failed to show up as expected for their scheduled gig.

Seven months after he first met Brian Jones and his band at the Marquee, Giorgio invited them to play at his club in Richmond, and only as a replacement for a band that had let him down. Moreover, the first concert of the Rollin' Stones at the Station Hotel was a complete fiasco with only three paying customers in attendance.

Eventually, Giorgio's club in the Station Hotel in the southwest London town of Richmond, which he first called the BR&B, for British Rhythm and Blues, became the legendary Crawdaddy Club that has earned a special place in rock history. Giorgio's pride was evident in the way he talked about these historical events encapsulated in this tiny newspaper clipping of the first concert of the Rollin' Stones at the Marquee.

Two other clippings announced concerts of the Rollin' Stones at the Station Hotel. They were personally prepared by Giorgio, who described them in superlative terms.

One described the band as "the thrilling, exhilarating,

GALVANIC, intoxicating, incomparable ROLLIN' STONES."

The other as "The craziest new RHYTHM 'N BLUES sound of the unparalleled ROLLIN' STONES."

I said to Giorgio: "You did not pull any punches." He did not answer, but gave me his most beautiful smile. His eyes sparkled and he suppressed a laugh.

Another clipping announced "DAVE HUNT'S R&B BAND every Sunday at 7.30 p.m. at the Richmond Hotel, RHYTHM & BLUES EXCITEMENT."

I admitted to Giorgio that I had never heard the name of this band before, and he told me, "It was the band of Ray Davies before he started the Kinks. Alexis Korner had sent them to me, and they played at my club before the Rolling Stones."

The last clipping was a simple message from Giorgio, who was in Switzerland with the Yardbirds, and who wished his friends and fans well for the next show of the T-Bones at the Crawdaddy.

Giorgio also showed me photographs of a young Eric Clapton, who was flashing a sly look in the company of Lord Ted Willis, the Home Secretary of the time. Giorgio had brought the Yardbirds to play for him on his birthday.

Lord Willis had just made some critical comments in

Parliament about British youth culture, and Giorgio saw fit to pay him an impromptu visit at his home with the band. Everything was amicable, and the Yardbirds got together with Giorgio and Lord Willis on the lawn of his house. But the concert was interrupted by the police after four songs because several neighbours had called to complain about the unbearable racket, which could be heard far and wide.

Thirty years later, Giorgio was still proud of this day, which he had organized and which proved a talking point for the Home Secretary, his neighbours, the Yardbirds, and himself. Finally, he showed me a photograph of the Yardbirds standing in a row with him behind Keith Relf and Eric Clapton. These photographs had been reproduced many times, but the ones he showed me seemed to be originals. Giorgio looked at them with obvious emotion.

I was totally in awe. If these clippings were only the start of his archives, what other gems were hidden in these drawers? Giorgio asked me to go and make photocopies of these clippings as he wanted to give them to one of his New York friends. I was happy to do it so that I could make extra copies for myself.

But this project promised to be a Herculean task, reminding me of the time, thirteen years earlier, when he had asked me to write his biography for him. Unfortunately, despite his good intentions, Giorgio never managed to organize his archives or write his memoirs.

***

I had succumbed to managing and playing in a new band called the Babas Cool, and organized some concerts in October 1996 in a Russian club located on 57th Street and Eleventh Avenue. I mentioned it to Giorgio and Scotty. Giorgio recommended that we do weekly shows on a regular basis, and Scotty volunteered once again to be our sound engineer. I booked the place for four Thursdays in a row, so we had to find a rehearsal space immediately.

I asked Giorgio to rent us time in the second floor rehearsal studio, but to my surprise, he told me that the studio was completely empty and that if I wanted to rent it, I would have to bring all of my own equipment. He explained that there had been several thefts of valuable equipment, that he had been forced to stop leaving anything in that room, and that he could no longer afford to replace what had been stolen.

He came to see us play at the Russian club anyway. We interpreted our own versions of old French rock songs by Les Chaussettes Noires, Les Chats Sauvages, Johnny Hallyday, et al. – all adaptations of American songs in the first place – and I was happy to see him support my efforts once again.

In June 1997, Scotty decided to marry his girlfriend. Giorgio had always acted like an older brother to Scotty too – sometimes even like a substitute father – and he organized a lunch in one of the private banquet rooms of the Gramercy Park Hotel, where he had spent several weeks when he came to New York in 1977.

This was a small, intimate gathering, and we were all happy for Scotty. But it was also a farewell to an old friend. Scotty had decided to return to the southern state where he had mysteriously come from ten years before. Scotty had always kept his earlier life private, and one of the rare mementos he had kept from his past was a large Confederate flag – the rebel flag – that he had hung on the wall of his room, which very few people had ever been invited to enter.

After the lunch, Scotty and I gave each other a big hug. A chapter was being closed in my own life right there and then, and I could see in Giorgio's eyes that he felt the same.

I never saw Scotty again. He left like he came, discretely, without a sound.

On April 19, 2000, the weekly paper *New York Press* published a very long interview with Giorgio, who described his international adventures in detail. I met him by chance in a French restaurant where he was having dinner with several members of L'Union Française, whom he still saw from time to time in spite of his demission from the lodge the year before. He had brought several copies of the paper, which featured a beautiful original portrait of a radiant Giorgio taken by Tom Legoff. It also featured copies of newspaper clippings that Giorgio had given them. It was truly great to watch Giorgio sitting, chatting amiably at this table, which was both friendly and fraternal.

On May 7, 2000, Giorgio produced an event at the Bowery Ballroom, *Rock in New York: The Sounds and the Stories,* which was sponsored by the New York Press. This event followed the theme of his old cable television show, for which he had interviewed important participants of the underground culture, like John Sinclair, who managed the band MC5; Marty Thau, who founded the indie punk movement in 1977 and who managed the New York Dolls; and Jim Fouratt, who was a militant of the Gay Liberation Front. The goal was to stream the event in netcasting on an internet channel, but unfortunately, this project did not go any further.

On September 26, 2000, Bob Gruen, the great rock photographer who had taken the famous shots of John Lennon in front of the Statue of Liberty, organized an exhibition of his photographs in the offices of MTV. Thanks to Giorgio's recommendation, Bob had agreed to be a member of the panel for my *Rock Search* program, which I had produced at Studio 54 on June 12, 1988, and after that, I saw him at Giorgio's parties from time to time.

Giorgio was there, of course, and I spent an excellent evening in their company. I was always happy to see them. One of the photographs in the exhibition was a portrait of John Lennon, and Bob explained to us how John enjoyed doing things out of the ordinary with him, even when they first met in 1972. Bob had showed up at the Record Plant Studio with his cameras as planned. He had been invited to document the recording of a new song, and he was naturally a bit anxious. Out of the blue, John invited him to sit on the floor of the sound booth to watch him sing and record the vocal track of "Woman Is the Nigger of the World."

Bob never forgot this first experience with John Lennon, and I could hear in his voice and see in his eyes the shiver of excitement he felt during the recording of the song as he was telling us this wonderful story, which Giorgio and I listened to with delight and respect.

Giorgio came to the Russian Samovar restaurant for dinner with Lilian and me on April 20, 2001. Lilian knew the owner well – his restaurant, located at 256 West 52nd Street, had been the meeting place for refugees from the old Soviet Union who came to America before its fall in 1991 – and

she had eaten there regularly since she came to New York in 1980.

The restaurant and the building were co-owned by several partners, including Mikhail Baryshnikov, and the second floor was often reserved for various literary and artistic groups for presentations in Russian, which always packed the room with those who were nostalgic for the old country,

Giorgio at Russian Samovar, 2001

157

even though they had been forced to leave on a one-way ticket with no possibility of ever returning due to political or religious reasons.

The restaurant also attracted writers like Norman Mailer, and painters whose artwork hung on the walls. Many Broadway singers, who were featured in Broadway shows in the neighbourhood, came here after work and improvised singsongs at the bar.

Giorgio loved the place, the food, and the atmosphere, as well as the owner Roman Kaplan, who spoke a little French, and whose naturally sophisticated style was only matched by his high sense of hospitality. It was also thanks to Roman who introduced me on July 20, 1989 to Lilian, that I met the woman who would become my future wife.

Unfortunately, with the passing of time, the old refugees of the former Soviet states became older and went out less often. The terrorist attacks on the Twin Towers on September 11, 2001 dented people's confidence too. The atmosphere of the place changed, Roman sold his shares, and we stopped going there by early 2004. New York never stands still and the new millenium had brought with it a realization that the city was not cut off from what was happening in the rest of the world. It would be more than ten years before the gaping wound at Ground Zero would be replaced with attractive memorial gardens.

***

To celebrate the 40th anniversary of the Rolling Stones, an independent production company decided to produce a documentary named *Just for the Record* for which they wanted to interview all kinds of people who had been involved, one way or another, in the life of the band. They called Giorgio, of course, and prepared a list of people to interview, setting up on the ground floor of Giorgio's house.

Giorgio invited me and Ronnie Bird on July 24, 2002, to meet the documentary producers from Los Angeles in case they wanted to hear what we had to say. I understood why he invited Ronnie, who was a natural since he opened for the Rolling Stones with his band during a European tour in the Spring of 1966, just as he had done for Chuck Berry the year before. His point of view as a French rock musician was therefore pertinent and interesting. But why should what I had to say matter?

I watched the six or seven people who were interviewed before me, and then my turn came. I was excited to be filmed and explained how their music had energised me since 1963. I was not convinced that my comments had added anything worthwhile to this long documentary, but when the 5 DVD box set was released, a friend of mine saw me on the video screen of a store in Greenwich Village, and he called me to

Ronnie Bird with Giorgio in Giorgio's house for his 77th birthday, 2011

tell me about it.

I ordered the box set, and I saw my contribution included between the interviews of Ronnie Bird and Anita Pallenberg in Chapter 5 of the first CD, which is dedicated to the 60s, and which is called "All the world's a stage."

When I first saw the Rolling Stones at the Olympia in Paris in 1965, I'd never have guessed in my wildest dreams that I'd be appearing in a documentary decades later to talk about them. The documentary was not an official production of the Rolling Stones. Mick Jagger and Keith Richards did not participate, but many other famous musicians and producers were interviewed and the documentary gave an extremely detailed account of the band's journey.

Four years later, Giorgio called me in February 2006. His friend Janice Daley worked for a company that sponsored the Robin Hood Foundation, an organization that helped underprivileged people in New York, and the Rolling Stones were going to give a concert at Radio City Music Hall to help the Foundation with a fundraiser. Did I want tickets?

These tickets were reserved for the employees of the companies that sponsored the event, as well as their friends

Giorgio with Janice Daley in Giorgio's house, 2009. Photo: Bob Gruen

and families, and the sponsoring companies gave the value of the tickets to Robin Hood. Janice could get me two, but I had to accompany her to the theatre. In order to stop scalpers, the tickets had to be left attached to the stub where the name of the employee was printed, so Lilian and I met Janice for the first time at this concert on March 14, 2006. With no explanation, Giorgio had decided that he did not want to go and see the band.

I had not seen the Rolling Stones in a real theatre since the concert of March 29, 1966, at the Olympia. I had seen them in large venues like the Palais des Sports in Paris, Cow Palace in San Francisco, the disastrous Altamont Speedway Free Festival near San Francisco, and Madison Square Garden, but this was a treat. Unlike stadiums where the sound was always muffled – like the last time I had seen them with Giorgio at Shea Stadium on October 28, 1989 – the sound at Radio City was crisp and balanced, and I could see the musicians without binoculars. A real pleasure.

Lilian and I never forgot that great night out with Janice. We warmed to her immediately. She was a kind person and we would see a lot more of her as she and Giorgio grew closer to each other. Surprisingly, Giorgio had met Janice on match.com and she became his partner for the last ten years of his life, caring for him as his health declined.

In March 2008, I contacted Giorgio for advice about a project I was contemplating. I wondered if I could make any money from the sale of the huge database of professional contacts for actors that I had compiled over the last twenty years. I was constantly sending mailings of postcards by the hundreds – sometimes by the thousands – to agents, producers, directors, and casting directors whose names and addresses I had gathered nationwide, and I updated this list systematically every week.

This extensive database was the tool that had best helped

me find work in the many branches of my profession, and I knew very well the value that this list had for actors who wanted to develop their network as I had done for myself. Selling it on the internet was a viable option for me, but I didn't know how to protect it from being copied and resold by others. I knew that there was something called digital rights management (DRM) that could provide me with the protection I needed, if I learned how to use it wisely. But I was a neophyte and so I called Giorgio to discuss it.

I met him at his place where he sat in the middle of a mountain of computers and video systems that were piled up on his console, and he explained to me what I had to do, which actually did not give me complete and guaranteed protection. He seemed to derive some kind of deviant pleasure from this, as he continued to believe that everything posted on the internet should be available for free for everybody in the world – the true democratization of knowledge in a modern world. But this was not what I had hoped for as I wanted to protect my intellectual property.

I thanked him and went back home a bit frustrated. I had to accept begrudgingly that I could not control everything – a lesson that Giorgio had been happy to teach me.

Giorgio offered his resources to the Obama presidential campaign, and I went to his house on August 28, 2008, to see and hear the speech of the Democratic candidate live on the internet and projected onto a huge screen. I was surprised to see the great number of young people who had gathered there and who seemed very interested in the possibility of our first Black president being elected.

Watching Obama and his wife Michelle, I was surprised that this racially mixed group of young people was mostly made up of young women. There was hope in the air that change would come about.

14. AND NOW, THE END IS NEAR...

"The music business is inhabited by people who have no
***king idea how to judge music."- GOMELSKY

On February 28, 2009, Giorgio celebrated his 75th birthday,
and as he had done every year, he threw a party at his house
and invited his friends. Nicole, Mamadou, Ronnie, Bob
Gruen, Rachid, Valerie Warner and her husband, and other
longtime friends like Larry Birnbaum. We all got together
under Giorgio's roof once again.

Giorgio always gave the bands who rehearsed in his
house a chance to play on the stage of the ground floor
before an audience. Sometimes, he also invited other New
York musicians to play, as he had with Jon Paris and Amy
Madden on his birthday in 2000.

I brought him a birthday gift, a black and white photo I had
found on the internet in which he was captured introducing
the Yardbirds on the stage of the Marquee in London on
March 20, 1964. I had ordered a nice print and bought a great
frame, and Giorgio really appreciated the thought, even if
the photo reminded him that the watch he was wearing in
the picture was the one his father had given him eons ago in
Switzerland, which he had managed to keep until the beautiful
Nico had stolen it to trade it for a bag of heroin.

Nico was a famous German singer who had first worked
as a model in Paris until she was discovered by Brian Jones
of the Rolling Stones. Later on, she became a protégée of

Andy Warhol and a member of the Velvet Underground (Lou Reed's band). She also tried to pursue her own solo singing career while sleeping at Giorgio's for a while.

This birthday party was special. The usual friends were there, but other unexpected guests showed up, like Steve van Zandt of Bruce Springsteen's E Street Band, who came to say hello. Giorgio went on stage to make a speech. First he complained about the "plumbing" problems that plagued people who reach a "certain age," then he went into his own musical presentation.

The Yardbirds had had a hit in October 1965 with "Still I'm Sad," the only Gregorian chant ever to climb the charts in England, and Giorgio had sung the bass part on the original recording. The sound engineer played the song and mixed down the vocals as much as possible, and Giorgio sang this bass part for us on his sound system.

He also reminded us that his voice could be clearly heard singing the "No" parts in "A Certain Girl" and that he was the one who, under the pseudonym of Oscar Rasputin, had written the instrumental "Got to Hurry," which had been played by the Yardbirds with a very young Eric Clapton.

Giorgio was as congenial as could be, but he actually had been suffering from serious health problems for at least a year. He was weak and had lost a lot of weight, and his physician recommended that he go back upstairs to his apartment to get some rest. He left us discretely after an hour or so and let the party go on without him.

Four months later, he organized a Bastille Day party at his house. It was a complete fiasco in spite of his good intentions. The first of the bands to play was a "noise" band that quickly got on most people's nerves. Everybody went out to the sidewalk where it was cooler, an older lady fainted on the sidewalk, an ambulance came to pick her up, guests and passers-by gathered to see what was happening, and the next-door neighbour, who had been complaining to the police for years about the noise that the bands made, called the cops. As the cops did not get there fast enough for her taste, she screamed at them and grabbed one by the arm. Two other cops forced her arms behind her back and handcuffed her, and since she refused to walk with them to the squad car, they picked her up and carried her away.

Giorgio sat like a Buddha on a chair by the entrance to the house, rolled a cigarette, and smoked it calmly. Lilian and I said goodbye and went home. I felt bad for him because he deserved better, but he did not seem to be bothered by what had just happened, as if we had just experienced another night in the long list of weird nights that the house had known. Tomorrow would be another day.

***

Life, the autobiography of Keith Richards, was released as a hardcover book in October 2010. I ordered two copies, one for me and one for Giorgio, and I went to see him with his copy the day I received it. Giorgio was 76 years old, but his eyes sparkled like a kid standing by the Christmas tree. He immediately went to the index, looked up his name, and read the paragraphs about him. He was content. What Keith wrote in the book was what Giorgio had told me for years. He felt vindicated and invigorated. The circle was complete, and I was happy to have been the one who brought him this ego booster and important tool of reinforcement. Besides, I would never be able to forget the expression on his face and the look in his eyes at this moment that mattered so much to him in his life.

However, I could not ignore the fact that the house had become completely uninhabitable. The next-door building had gone through major repairs, and the side of a wall had crumbled and fallen onto the roof of his house. There were now several holes through which rainwater gushed in. Giorgio had raised a few plastic sheets to shelter some areas from the water, and we were sitting under one of these as if we were in a refugee camp. The image of a happy Giorgio reading what Keith had written about him, while we sat in this apocalyptic setting, will stay with me forever.

This did not prevent him from inviting friends to his 77th birthday party on February 27, 2011. It was an intimate gathering. Nicole, Ronnie, my wife Lilian, and a half-dozen other people were there. It was actually like a family affair in a strange way, and everybody seemed to be having a good time even though the mood was rather subdued. Giorgio's elder daughter, Alexandra, had come from England and was there with her partner and their three children. It was the first time that Giorgio had met her and her partner together with his three grandchildren in New York. He seemed happy to be given the opportunity to get to know his grandchildren, and he asked me to take a family portrait in which he really looked radiant.

Giorgio with Nicole Devilaine, February 27, 2011

We were old friends getting together and catching up with each other, and we were also old friends who were obviously getting older too. Most of us had known each other for thirty years, and we had been in our mid-thirties to early forties when we had first met. We got together as often as possible here in this house – most of us were immigrants who had arrived in this great city with the same hopes and dreams that generations of immigrants had had before us.

We could all see that Giorgio was not well, but he carried on smoking his cigarettes as if everything was fine, despite the fact that, as we later learned, he was suffering from colon cancer.

It was a few months later that Ronnie called me to tell me that Giorgio had been hospitalized and that the surgeons had removed a tumour from his stomach. Lilian and I rushed to the hospital, where Ronnie, Nicole Devilaine, Janice Daley, and Valerie Warner and her husband were already by Giorgio's side.

It turned out that Giorgio had been seriously ill at home for several weeks but that he had refused to go to a hospital in spite of the terrible pain.

Raul Gonzalez, a musician of the mariachi-punk band Barra Libre, who was managing things at the house, smelled something horrible coming from Giorgio's apartment, went up to see what was going on, and found him in an awful state. Raul called the emergency services right away.

I went to see Giorgio as often as possible. He was recuperating in his hospital bed, and since he often complained about the food, Ronnie cooked him better and tastier fare at home to improve his diet. Giorgio was taking painkillers because of the post-operative pain, and I found him more congenial than he had been in a long time. We talked about all our adventures – and he recommended that I write down my memories because my life had been unique for a Frenchman born and raised in France. I listened to his advice, then actually started writing two months later, and that was how my book *Expat New York* came to life.

After a long recovery in a convalescent home, Giorgio returned to his dilapidated house, which by then, the social services had officially declared unlivable. How he managed to get back in, nobody knew.

Curiously enough, 2013 was an active year for his "legacy." On January 19, an article about him was published in the *New York Times* and, on April 30, on the Truth Is Cool website. All this would have been much more helpful twenty years earlier, but Giorgio appreciated this belated recognition. Better late than never.

Giorgio managed to organize more private parties in his dilapidated house. Having observed a similar concept at one of his friend's homes in Greenwich Village, he organized an interview with Jesse Malin, one of the few New York musicians who had rehearsed in his house during the days of Paddles, when the Volcanos and Surgery were rehearsing alternately with his band. Giorgio hoped that the experience would be successful enough to be repeated, and he gave the name of Oh Blah Blah to this new series.

Jesse Malin was an important figure in the underground music scene of New York City. His first band, Heart Attack, was started when he was only twelve years old, but that did not prevent them from auditioning at CBGB, where they could not be booked because of their age, since the musicians and their fans would not have been allowed to be served at the bar.

Heart Attack lasted from 1979 to 1984. Jesse continued to play and record with many musicians until he started coming to Giorgio's, where he met other musicians with whom he started D Generation in 1991, a band that became successful until their breakup in 1999.

I realized during the interview that Giorgio had recommended that Jesse follow our example of playing at house parties which was not surprising since we always had full houses and generated positive cash flow. But starting in 1991, Jesse Malin, Howie Pyro, and Holly Ramos pushed the envelope much further when they started their Green Door Parties, which became a magnet for the followers of the New York underground. I was actually happy to hear Jesse speak of those days and remind everybody that this place used to harbour an S&M club called Paddles, which made it possible for Giorgio to keep the house that our bands badly needed for rehearsals.

Unfortunately, only fifteen people showed up for the video recording of Giorgio's interview with Jesse, and I was rather sad to see that Giorgio's star had waned.

As usual, Giorgio did not seem downcast and he explained that the Oh Blah Blah series was his own way of recording his own memories as well as those of the artists he had worked with for so long so that an oral history of

Jesse Malin with Giorgio. Photo: Bob Gruen c.2005

rock could be preserved in the words of those who had actually lived it.

He had already interviewed more than thirty people: artists, managers, club owners, writers, and DJs, as well as ordinary people who witnessed key moments in the history of rock in New York. He wanted to do the same in London and Paris, and when he had finished with rock, he would do the same with jazz and the avant-garde movements in a series that he would call, of course, "Ohblahblah," to be streamed on the internet, the perfect medium for this kind of project. He ended with the thought that, in spite of everything, he had always done his best, and that, as long as he was still here...

The date of this event with Jesse Malin in the house at 140 West 24th Street in Manhattan was December 13, 2012. That was the last time I saw Giorgio.

***

On February 28, 2013, several friends and musicians – including the Hispanic marketing director Raul Gonzalez, the photographer Ian Cuttler, and the sound engineer Nils Svensson – decided to start the Red Door Collective group as a fundraiser to restore the house, which had never fully recovered from the collapse onto its roof of the side wall from the building next door.

They wanted to raise $25,000 in 35 days, and 103 donors stepped up to the plate to meet this goal. Plans were drawn up and repair work actually started, but it quickly became obvious that much more money was needed for the house to be safe enough to let people in. A heavy rainfall set back the restoration project when it caused more damage, and City Hall finally declared the house condemned once and for all.

Before the vacate notices were posted on the entrance door, a last party was organized on May 15, 2015, by the Red Door Collective, with a multimedia presentation to honour

Giorgio and the legendary place that he had made available for New York artists during the previous thirty-seven years. Bob Gruen, Dave Soldier, and Gary Lucas took turns and presented an oral history, followed by a concert with Gary Lucas, a guitar player whose career included Captain Beefheart, Lou Reed, Jeff Buckley, Nick Cave, Chris Cornell and David Johansen – and his band Gods and Monsters.

Giorgio sat in front of a portrait of himself that had been recently painted on one of the walls and listened to all the tributes. It was an eery sight, as though he was presiding over his own funeral. The idea of the event was to give him a living memorial and I hope he felt the love and appreciation from all who were gathered there – it was a moving experience for all involved.

At the time of the May 15, 2015 farewell party for the house, Giorgio had already moved to an apartment that he

Giorgio sitting next to his portrait painted on a wall
on May 15, 2015. Photo: Bob Gruen

Raul Gonzalez at the service for Giorgio, February 27, 2016

could not really afford on 12th Street and Avenue A. Old friends, family and former partners helped with the expenses, and Giorgio lived there modestly. Few friends passed by to pay him a visit. Janice Daley, whom Nicole called a "true saint," continued to take care of him, but his health slowly deteriorated, and he had to be placed in a Medicare-certified nursing home in the Bronx, the Calvary Hospital Hospice, located at 1740 Eastchester Road, where he passed away on January 13, 2016, at 3:45 a.m. from complications caused by his colon cancer, as Janice told the *New York Times* for his obituary.

January 13th happens to be my birthday, so I will never be able to forget the date of his departure to the other side. Several obituaries were published including in *The New York Times, The Telegraph, The Guardian,* and *The Scotsman.*

The last of his friends to see him was Raul Gonzalez,

who still does not know what has really become of Giorgio's prized possessions after they were removed from the house when it was condemned by the City of New York.

Will the huge video archive recorded by Giorgio, with dozens of interviews for the purpose of creating the encyclopedia of rock as he lived it, ever see the light of day? And under what conditions? Or will it remain the best-kept secret of his generation?

Raul organized a memorial service on February 27, 2016 at St Marks Church-in-the-Bowery, located at 131 East 10th Street, and I organized on April 19, 2016 a moment of remembrance at L'Union Française, where I played "You Gotta Move" and "Amazing Grace" on a blues harmonica in his memory.

Through research for this book I learned of Giorgio's final resting place. His ashes were interred in the Wust family plot number 1-PBE-51-/ alongside his mother in the cemetery in Monaco. He had always hoped to return to the French Riviera someday, and his daughter Donatella was able to grant this final wish.

Giorgio's final resting place in the cemetery in Monaco

On August 20, 2017, Larry Birnbaum, distinguished music writer and editor, sent me the following message.

Recollection by Larry Birnbaum

"Before I met Giorgio Gomelsky, I knew he had managed the Yardbirds and the early Rolling Stones, so as a longtime Stones and Yardbirds fan, I was slightly in awe of him when we were first introduced at one of his Red Door Parties. I was flattered that he took me seriously as a critic and (at that time) world music radio disc jockey; he even had me bring some African CDs to subsequent parties.

Giorgio was always ahead of the curve, which may have hindered his later career. He was a devotee of Amiga computer software, and before DSL lines became common, he could hardly stop talking about this new technology that would allow live concerts to be transmitted in real time. I admired his youthful spirit and the way he kept up with trends, musical and otherwise. I once bumped into him riding his bicycle down a busy Manhattan avenue when he was in his seventies.

Giorgio seemed to know everyone in the music business. At one of his parties, I met the outlaw poet John Sinclair, who used to manage the MC5, an avant-rock band whom I saw give an unforgettable performance at a protest of the 1968 Democratic Party convention in Chicago.

Giorgio never lost his taste for the blues, which he had acquired in England in the late 1950s. I remember that he attended a concert by the legendary Mississippi Delta bluesman Honeyboy Edwards not long before Edwards' death in 2011. And he would insist that the Yardbirds were essentially a blues band. It was his love for the blues that led him to become what Keith Richards called the "de facto manager" of the Rolling Stones, getting them press coverage and booking some of their earliest gigs. What I didn't know was that Giorgio was also instrumental in launching the career of the Kinks' leader Ray Davies.

Giorgio helped bring about a musical and cultural revolution through his early promotion of the Stones, who not only changed the course of rock 'n' roll but had an enormous impact on fashion and public attitudes. By thumbing their noses at convention, the Stones inspired a generation of young rebels whose dress, hairstyles and musical preferences reflected the Stones' influence. The Yardbirds pushed the musical envelope still further, paving the way for psychedelic rock and heavy metal.

Giorgio later worked with many other progressive musicians, from Julie Driscoll and Brian Auger to Soft Machine, Henry Cow, Bill Laswell, Material and the Czech band Plastic People of the Universe. He continued to present up-and-coming rockers at Red Door, the performance space on the ground floor of his residence.

When I was the editor of a book imprint, I suggested to Giorgio that he write an autobiography. Unfortunately, he never did, for he surely had many tales to tell.

An illustrious music industry mover and shaker, Giorgio Gomelsky has earned a place of honor in the history of an era that saw a major transformation of society.

We owe him a debt of gratitude."

– Larry Birnbaum

Larry Birnbaum, 2017

On August 21, 2017, photographer and long-time associate of Giorgio, Bob Gruen, sent me the following message.

Recollection by Bob Gruen

"I always thought of Giorgio as my professor of advanced sociology, the study of human behavior and culture. He loved to talk about just about anything and how it related to everything and to all of us. Giorgio always looked like a professor, with a European sense of style, usually wearing an academic-looking sport jacket, shirt with collar, and trousers. He had an artists' instructor look about him.

I first met Giorgio in the late 70s at the Tramps bar on East 15th Street, near the corner of Irving Place. It was a typical neighborhood Irish bar meant for serious drinking. Since it was next door to a Sailors' Union old age home, there were always a few veteran sailors sitting at the end of the bar sipping shots and beer. But Tramps' owner Terry Dunne, with agent Steve Weitzman, booked bluesmen from the South, New Orleans in particular, including some famous names like Big Joe Turner. Giorgio loved the blues, and Tramps had a regular supply of real live blues. My friend David Johansen and I started to make Tramps a regular spot after Max's Kansas City nearby became too crowded. As Giorgio started to become a regular visitor too, we got to talking to him and soon became friends with him.

He was relatively new to New York but never talked about where he came from. He seemed to know things about London and Paris, but he didn't talk about his past. Giorgio talked about the future and its possibilities for all people. He had great faith in the power of the arts to move public opinion for the betterment of society and never tired of talking to people to work out various intelligent ways to get the message across.

There was some mystery about where Giorgio came from. There were rumors that he had something to do with the music scene in London, and before that Paris, but for years I knew nothing of his background because he never mentioned it. Then one night in the early 80s, Lowell Fulson was playing at Tramps and Mick Jagger came to see him. On his way in, he saw Giorgio at the bar, and Mick stopped to give him a big hug and happy "hello" and stayed to talk for a while. When we saw how friendly they obviously were, I realized some of the rumors I heard about Giorgio were true.

Over the years I found out a lot more. He was a friend of Serge Gainsbourg in Paris and helped him get connected in London. Giorgio had gone there first and he started the coffeehouse movement because he wanted espresso instead of tea in London. He convinced his boss to open a coffeehouse so people could have a place to go to talk after the pubs closed, which was at 9 p.m. at that time, and then he took that further and had bands play there. He gave the Rolling Stones their first-ever shows because he liked the blues. He showed the Beatles around London and then gave them the idea for *A Hard Day's Night*. He started and managed the Yardbirds, and later his all-time favorite band, Magma. Finding these things out came a few sentences at a time over many years because he had no interest in talking about his past. Giorgio was much more interested in the future.

He was an honest and sincere critic, giving the kind of advice that bands, artists, and friends didn't always agree with at first but later thanked him for. He loved to listen to people and hear their opinions and then give his views and discuss the differences for hours. Giorgio could be very insistent on his point of view and could be very aggressive in trying to get someone to understand that.

He was a connoisseur but not a snob. He could accept and enjoy whatever he got, but he had an expert understanding of what was good or what was not. He enjoyed good food and wine and was a very good cook himself.

He seemed to have a great knowledge of many subjects as diverse as politics, artists, writers, recipes, and many other things. That was part of why it was so interesting to talk to Giorgio, because he knew the history of something, how it came to be and where it was now and what it could become.

His loft space became a center for the arts. The second and third floors he semi-soundproofed and rented out as rehearsal rooms at very low rates to local bands to give them a place to get a start. Along with the low rent came lots of free advice on how to advance their grand ambitions. He opened the street level floor as a large performance space and put a stage at the end to have endlessly varied nights with people holding all kinds of events, from local political meetings, poetry readings, book discussions, and avant-garde theater and dance, to band parties (and for a while, a private S&M club rented the place once a month for their "meetings").

You never knew what you would find or who you would meet at Giorgio's, but you had a good idea that something interesting or just weird would happen there. Often Giorgio would be stirring a big kettle of some spiced cider with an assortment of liquors to warm the hearts and minds of the

Giorgio with Bob Gruen

intellectuals and oddballs who met at his events.

That's the way I remember him, stirring things to get people to talk to each other and work out differences and create new and better ways of doing things."

– Bob Gruen

On August 19, 2017, musician and mentee of Giorgio, Jesse Malin sent me a message.

Recollection by Jesse Malin

"I first met Giorgio when I was 15 years old at a wacky weekly music series he was doing at CBGB called Tonka Wonka Mondays. At that time I was way into hardcore punk and could not relate to this eclectic, kooky mix of jams he and his fellow DJs were bringing forth, but something about Giorgio stood out, for sure.

A few months later, me and my girlfriend were invited to a Bastille Day party at his Chelsea loft. He made a huge soup and had all these cool guests, like David Johansen and Richard Hell. Giorgio was very funny with all of them, goofing around the whole place, which looked like the party scene in *Midnight Cowboy.*

He even got down and did a comedy bit with David Johansen on a couch, with Giorgio playing the shrink and David as the patient.

It all felt a bit over our heads, but definitely got us intrigued. We loved hearing him, in his thick, untraceable, deep, dark accent, greet Richard Hell as "Ricardo Inferno" when he arrived. We had some of his soup, and Giorgio grunted a few things at us.

A month or so later, I found myself playing a show with my teen hardcore band Heart Attack at that very same loft, which now appeared to be a live venue. We were told that Giorgio lived upstairs and rented the rest of the place out to musicians on a daily basis to rehearse and even put on shows there. We also heard that Giorgio had once managed the Rolling Stones, produced the Yardbirds, and given Eric Clapton his nickname, Slowhand. This guy was getting more interesting by the minute.

He took a liking to our band, gave us some wacky advice, and offered up his place to us any time we needed it. He was blunt, brisk, and brutally honest. There was also something very warm about him. We had no idea where he was really from, but my drummer in his youthful ignorance would refer to him as "the Russian."

We took him up on his offer when we had nowhere to play one New Year's Eve in 1982. That night, we quickly learned how to put on a show outside of a real club. With the help of our friends the False Prophets, we invited MDC, the Misguided, Reagan Youth, and many others to play. It would also be the first ever Murphy's Law show they would ever play. We brought in our own beer, gear, and door person, and even learned how to pay off the cops when they eventually showed up.

Giorgio loved it and told stories about Swinging London and the Crawdaddy Club back in the 60s as he drank way into the wee hours. We left after sunrise and actually made a few bucks. It was one of the first of many lessons I learned from Giorgio and his magic spot at 140 West 24th Street.

Years would pass but sometimes I would see him at shows or when I was a moving man and I had to load in an all-girl punk-polka band called Das Fürlines who were rehearsing there. It was Saturday night and we had to navigate the gear through an S&M party that was there called Paddles. To be clear, it wasn't Giorgio throwing the party or participating; he was only renting his space out to them. He was probably upstairs banging away at his computer (and this is years before the cyber times – he was always way ahead) while I was rolling the big bass amp and drums in through the tied up, paddled patrons.

One December day in 1990, me and some close friends were trying to come up with a way to spend another New Year's Eve and not be in some big, dumb corporate rock club. We wanted to play records that were not heard on the radio or at clubs and get people to dress up, dance, and go crazy.

I suddenly thought of Giorgio's spot and gave him a ring. For $400 we could have the place till sunrise and do anything we wanted. We needed a name, and the door was painted green, so contrary to unpopular belief, that's how we got the name the GreenDoorNYC.

The night was a success, and we all had such a blast, people begged us to do another one. Suddenly, it became a monthly affair. As broke musicians, it paid our bills while we tried to get our band off the ground, and we were having a blast. Now I could do fewer back-breaking moving jobs and more rehearsing.

Eventually we would play our first show there as D Generation. The party got so big we had to move into a larger space, which would become my first experience opening a legal (well sorta) nightclub. D Generation would soon land a major record deal and go on to world touring (believe it or not). We would still rehearse at Giorgio's place and even had our big tour bus pick us up there. He would break our balls, say that we played too loud, and put us in check whenever our egos got too big, but in the end he would always wish us the best of luck. On our first album, we used a voicemail message from Giorgio to open up one of the songs. Years later he would also make a special appearance narrating the intro of my video for "Broken Radio," a song I recorded with Bruce Springsteen, written about my mother, who had passed away way too young.

Giorgio would always say in his big and wild accent that his loft was our *la-bor-a-tory* to create and experiment in. I think back to so many of his ideas: a remake of the musical *West Side Story* set in 1983 that would take place on the Lower East Side with "Hardcore Kids vs. Hip-Hop Kids," his version of *The Producers* called *Elvis in Space*, a 25 minute mix of a song I had called "Riding on the Subway," the oral history of rock (filmed by him), a naked protest called "Asses across America" (starting on Fifth Avenue at 5 a.m.), and a plan for me to open up a delicatessen called Jesse's that would have every kind of food from every nationality.

I felt horrible when I heard that he had lost that place. Around that time, his health was declining, but his spirit remained intact. Even on his final days in the hospital, he was still giving me hell, but also letting me know, in his own way, that he was happy to see me.

Without Giorgio's generosity, guidance and tough criticism, I would truly not be the person I am today. I miss him dearly. Wherever he actually came from – France, Italy, Russia, England, Mars – Giorgio was a rare gem of a human being whose spirit will always remain with me."

– Jesse Malin

Malin at the Bowery Ballroom, 2015
Photo: gsstoll

In the Winter of 1981-1982, Giorgio gave me a 12" EP of two songs that he had just produced for the band A Blind Dog Stares on his new record label Guillotine Records (A cut above the rest). I recently managed to get in touch with Brad Rim, the lead singer of the band, who sent me this text and photo in an email dated December 21, 2022.

Recollection by Brad Rim

"The dawn of the 1980s was a surreal period to be young and coming-of-age in New York City. Although there was a certain amount of peaceful tranquility (no active wars or drafts), there was a very palpable recession-era undercurrent of dark edginess and significant amounts of urban decay. It is in this pre-gentrified, pre-MTV early 80s urban environment that my alternative rock band A Blind Dog Stares started working with him and rehearsing at his studio/residence called *Plugg* on West 24th Street in Manhattan.

Under Gomelsky's influence, twice a week at his dimly-lit and spooky *Plugg* rehearsal studios, my band's music went from punky, mod-revivalism to nearly full-on Gong-like Euro-abstraction in a scant six months. Giorgio pushed us into interesting and somewhat uncomfortable musical zones, but it somehow worked for me. Thus, we hired him to produce our first 12" independent single "Thru the Fence" and even threw him a nod with the B-side covering a crazy Ghostbusters-like Gong song he previously produced, "Troller Tanz".

Amazingly, this 12" single peaked at #3 on CMJ's definitive college radio charts – an awesome feat considering college radio was the only outlet for a young, underground rock band to get any recognition or airplay in 1981/82. At the time, I recall thinking that Giorgio didn't have much to do with the record's success at this alternative level, but in hindsight, he was a masterful teacher pushing my creativity away from the pop-rock prosaic and towards perhaps a more thoughtful and abstracted zone. Listening to it today, the record sounds quite dark, abstract and moody, and for me it's still a tough listen, but it really does conjure up that moody, surreal, darkish environment of very early 1980s Manhattan.

Moody, surreal and dark, was the Giorgio I remember from that period. A man of intense intellectual and artistic commentary, fuelled by a good bourbon (or two, or three or four!), sitting at the bar at Tramps on East 15th Street along with his music producer friend Marty Thau, holding court to a bevy of youth, a generation younger than him. I recall a man who never thought twice about how he wanted to live his life and was never interested in compromising or really dovetailing with the status quo of the time.

Time passed, I moved on to Los Angeles, came back and last saw Giorgio riding his bicycle on West 23rd Street in 1989. He hardly recognized me as I had joined the corporate world by then, walking around in my London fog raincoat as a newly minted 30-year-old advertising agency Yuppie. He didn't seem to disapprove though. I think he knew that only a scant few could live the alternative life that he had chosen and that the rest of us eventually would morph into

that classic "How to identify a Yuppie" poster that National Lampoon had made famous in the day.

Giorgio was that perfect alternative, underground character appearing in that perfect, alternative, wonderful period of New York City, 1980."

– Brad Rim

Brad Rim, 1982

Inducted into the New York City Blues Hall of Fame on August 19, 2022, Amy Madden is known for having played her masterful bass guitar with the likes of John Lee Hooker and Johnny Winter. She is also a published poet and author. I have seen her play bass with the Jon Paris Trio in various venues of New York City over the years, and at Giorgio's house for his 66th birthday on February 28, 2000. Amy was a good friend of Giorgio's for decades, and I received her recollection by email on January 19, 2023, just in the nick of time for the publication of this book.

Recollection by Amy Madden

I first met Giorgio at the old Tramps on 15th Street while Terry Dunne was the owner; Giorgio was kind of the ringmaster. The sound of his voice tracks every memory I have of that club. I guess I'd been to Newport as a teenager, but jazz and blues had been eclipsed by my fascination with CBGB's, the New York Lower East Side rock scene. Jon Paris re-introduced me to the blues in the late 70s. We often double dated with Johnny and Susan Winter, and at Tramps I was initiated into the select audience of people like Cedell Davis and Big Joe Turner. All of these memories are like old black and white negatives, colorized by Giorgio – this bearded man literally exploding with enthusiasm and information. There aren't many people from this scene that you refer to by one name only.

When I began playing bass, he often showed up at Dan Lynch's or the Lone Star – part of his night-crawls to sate his ever-insatiable passion for good music... new or old. Blues, he taught me, was the real alternative scene in New York City. He was there when I backed up John Lee Hooker at the Limelight – the night I was initiated into the true blues canon. It was a revelation.

I was fortunate to be on Giorgio's regular guest list for birthdays and events at the Green Door where you'd witness him holding court in his element. There was always something going on – he'd take us upstairs and show us how he was making a film, or he'd be virtually overflowing with enthusiasm about some new band or project. There were people there from all 'scenes'... he was a cross-pollinator... he made sure the young bands were drinking and jamming in the room with the old guard. Sometimes he'd be bartending... sometimes he'd be doling out his famous minestrone. He was an incomparable host. Jon and I played one or two of his parties alongside glam and punk bands. He was especially welcoming to my songwriting and listened to cassettes and scolded me for not embracing my solo career. There was always some young woman bassist or guitarist around and he'd put our heads together and expect some mentoring to come out of it.

Occasionally, over the years, I'd stop by his building – sometimes wheeling my baby boy in a stroller – and I'd always come away with determination, energy. He was contagious. He was electric and more alive than almost anyone I ever met. If there was a new musical pie, his thumb was in it.

At the last party, he was upstairs, ill. Janice was graciously hosting in his place. There were problems with the building. The gentrification of the city had eaten up so much of the old urban energy. It was worrying... I kept looking upstairs, thinking he'd appear. People like Giorgio appear. Not frequently, not anymore.

No one was prepared for his death. It was a generational wound for us musicians, in a way, like the death of John Lennon in New York City. The St. Mark's memorial service on his birthday eve was long and the performers and speakers were diverse. Most of us were too sad and stunned to think of performing. Terry Dunne was there... he was palpably sad. We felt wounded, grieved... aged. No one like this was ever going to cross our paths. No one was going to kick our butts and teach us about these moments in life, or make sure we crossed musical boundaries without prejudice, with humility and passion. He was a musical activist, Giorgio. A catalyst. And yet he was solid. He was history; he bridged musical generations and genres. He had vision. He changed me. Just thinking about him now makes me want to pick up a guitar and create something, because that is the only way to honour his spirit.

A young filmmaker who was documenting the downtown scene came to say hello after the memorial service. "I didn't know you knew Giorgio," I said. "I didn't," she said, "but I knew I had to be here."

I guess Giorgio would have agreed.

— Amy Madden

Amy Madden. Photo: Leland Bobbé, 2016

Raul Gonzalez, musician and close friend of Giorgio, sent me this message on September 3, 2017.

Recollection by Raul Gonzalez

"I first came across the name Giorgio Gomelsky in Led Zeppelin's unauthorized biography, *Hammer of the Gods*, which I was reading with great enthusiasm in the summer of 2005 shortly after my recently formed band in New York City, Barra Libre, was beginning to make some noise. As a guitarist, singer and songwriter playing in a band since I first took on rock 'n' roll in Mexico City in the early 90s, I always had great admiration for the bands that came from the blues in the early 60s in England, like the Yarbdirds and Rolling Stones.

Growing up in Mexico, we always listened to American and British rock, and when I formed my first band there, we discovered the Yardbirds and their sense of musical adventure, extended jams, and inclusion of world music elements. So we started doing the same, injecting some of our own Latin grooves and culture into our rock 'n' roll, while still following the beat of the 60s British bands who were gods to us. That path took us to Boston, where my band played for five years and eventually broke up. With a bit of musical heartbreak, I then moved to New York City in 2000 with a job in entertainment PR, and soon my brother, who had been the drummer of my band, moved to New York as well. Naturally, we started jamming and before we knew it, we had formed another band, Barra Libre, a playful party term that in Spanish means "open bar."

As I found myself once again on the rock 'n' roll path, I was fascinated with Led Zeppelin and knowing how it had actually emerged from the Yardbirds, and this moved me to read *Hammer of the Gods*. What I did not expect was that I would soon cross paths with the man largely responsible for it all – Giorgio. Landing at his events space on 24th Street unexpectedly one night was one of those occasions where synchronicity in the universe happens.

It was on Halloween night of 2005 that Barra Libre was booked to play a late night set at a party that was being hosted by a fabulous comedy rock band called Bad Teenage Moustache. They were looking for another band to play a late set and had put an ad on craigslist that I responded to, and we got booked. When we arrived at the party space on 24th Street, there was great energy in what looked like a CBGB seedy venue, very punk rock, and everyone was dressed up in costume. We played a set that included our signature high energy blend of "mariachi-punk," and the crowd went wild. The party was loud and crazy and it felt like the right type of rock 'n' roll place where it can get a little dangerous.

The next day, Danny from Bad Teenage Moustache called me to thank my band for playing and also to tell me that the owner of the place, Giorgio, wanted to meet us because he liked what he heard from my band last night. He said that Giorgio was an old producer who once in the 60s had a role with the Rolling Stones. I wasn't too impressed. After all, it was New York City, and everyone was somebody with some exaggerated story. His name sounded somewhat familiar, but at the time I did not connect the fact that it was because he was in the book I had been reading a few months ago. We gratefully accepted the invitation to meet him, and me and my bandmates went to his apartment that evening, which was on the top floor of the building where the party had been.

My first impression of Giorgio was that of a sweet, grandfatherly figure who loved to talk a lot. And even though the conversation was not even about music at first, I found it to be very engaging and thought that he was an unusually cultured person. He also seemed genuinely interested in the fact that most of the band was from Mexico and wanted to know about our culture, so we talked and talked.

After about four hours, he finally told us why he wanted to meet us. He said that he thought he could help my band and offered us his house as a rehearsal space if we agreed to take his guidance as a sort of producer. In a very humble manner, he then told us about the Rolling Stones and him managing the Yardbirds, and stories with the Beatles. We were flattered, but at the same time we didn't really believe him and were a bit skeptical about taking his offer, even though he seemed very nice and undoubtedly intelligent.

That night when I got home, it occurred to me: What if Giorgio was in fact telling the truth and was one of the characters I read about in *Hammer of the Gods*? I immediately picked up the book and started skimming through the first pages where the band was being formed, and there it was, Jimmy Page himself talking about Giorgio Gomelsky, and then a few more pages on Gomelsky's management of the Yardbirds. My heart pounded, and I knew this was destiny.

We took Giorgio's offer, and he started coming to some of our shows and giving us all kinds of feedback and advice, some of which we took, some we didn't. He thought that we should dress up in Aztec costumes and pay tribute by playing an Aztec tribal groove. We said we weren't ready for that yet. He also suggested that our first release should be recorded live, as he did with the Yardbirds. That we did. We tracked most of it live under Giorgio's supervision, and then we did some overdubs. He was enthusiastic about the fact that Barra Libre had several world music elements and that we especially loved playing African beats. We had one song called "All Fall Down" that had an Afro-funk beat that Giorgio really liked. That opened a conversation with him that lasted many years, about the origin of most music today being from Africa, and as such, he gave me a very thick book, *Cuba and Its Music*, by Ned Sublette, which I still have not finished.

He taught us some truly fascinating techniques and had amazing observations on how to put together an "irresistible set," as he'd call it. He also employed some pretty interesting teachings, like Mr. Miyagi from *The Karate Kid.* One day he called us for an early rehearsal, and as we arrived, there were two rolls of carpet, hammers, nails, and glue guns. He wanted us to recarpet all the stairs and showed us the method to work as a team, convincing us that by doing this and getting all the corners right, we'd improve on our tightness as a band and our attention to detail. He also repeatedly told us, "If you serve the music, the music will serve you." We had many interpretations of that, and it is not until many years later that I truly came to understand what he meant and how right he was.

Under his guidance, we started doing monthly shows/parties at his event space that at the time was called the Purple Door and soon became Red Door. He had the idea of growing an "intelligent audience" by selecting and inviting like-minded people who were interested in the music and culture and who were not just going to be there to get drunk and try to get girls. He was also very interested in technology and the internet, and so to do this we employed some early social media marketing using Myspace, which was the trend before Facebook became popular. I would sit with Giorgio for hours, showing him how to use Myspace to filter through profiles of people who liked similar music artists, and he always had ideas on how to invite people. On one of the first shows we did at his venue, he even printed questionnaires that he handed out to people and asked them to write answers about their musical taste and what they thought of the band. I have to admit that it was probably not very effective, as this new millennial audience was not really into filling out surveys at a party. But that was Giorgio, and he was always ready (and stubborn) to try out different ideas. But no matter what, he always wanted us to listen to and play Captain Beefheart.

After two years of working with Giorgio, Barra Libre took a hiatus and eventually ended. For me, however, it seemed that the music kept chasing me, and for the next eight years or so, I stayed by Giorgio's side, becoming his right-hand man, managing his music space, doing events and music there, and more importantly, becoming good friends with him. I lived only a few blocks away, so I was there for long hours every day. During those first couple of years, he became an incredibly important mentor who helped me through many aspects of my personal life, music endeavors, and even in my professional career, which is in PR for pro football/soccer. Giorgio was a huge soccer aficionado and a big Chelsea FC supporter. He had such incredible knowledge and understanding of the beautiful game, that to an extent, he also served as my advisor on several of my soccer projects.

It was also on this plane that we seemed to understand each other well, as we always saw music much like a soccer game, with some of the same basic principles applying to both. It was all about the groove. He explained how several soccer team tactics were the same in music and vice versa, and it made complete sense. Much in the same manner that soccer is universal, he saw music as universal and global, so there was always a juxtaposition of the two in his philosophy of how soccer and music served as part of civilization, and how they should groove. Just as in soccer, where the best club teams are the ones who get players from different countries and adopt diverse playing styles, he believed that the best music also came from such cultural mixes, just as the blues had come from Africa and then lent itself to British R&B. He felt that the future of music was global and universal, and he thus was very much interested in the whole Latin thing, because even though he didn't know much about it, he knew that its influence on Western culture was growing faster than ever.

In a way, he was also like my therapist, and so to an extent, he successfully helped me in defining my identity. He was really great with that, and many people would come to him for that. Indeed, he loved to talk and be the charmer, but he also loved to listen and take in a lot with authentic interest.

In 2012, Giorgio and I, with another two friends of mine, formed the Red Door Collective, with the aim of restoring his house (Red Door), reviving it with music events and creating something relevant again. We raised funds through a Kickstarter campaign and embarked on a mission that we realized was too big of an undertaking. We were able to fix a lot of stuff, but certainly not all of the problems, and indeed temporarily revived the place with electrifying events, live music, and incubating experimental artists of all sorts. One such artist was the band City of the Sun. I brought them in, and in addition to letting them rehearse there, Giorgio actually allowed them to live in a small room with a bed for six months or so, as these very young guys were actually homeless. But they were very good, playing a mix of high-energy flamenco punk that ensured us a packed house every time they performed. Giorgio would try to advise them and referred to them as the "bohemians" because they didn't want to listen much and just floated around a bit carelessly with their God-given talent, playing good music, sometimes sloppy, but getting a lot of girls. After they left the Red Door, sure enough, City of the Sun went on to become a successful touring band, playing pretty big shows, and now they are a quite popular new band on the rise.

The last four years of Giorgio's life were indeed difficult for him and most of us close to him because his health was deteriorating, and with it, his temperament as well. He would become increasingly agitated with everything and everyone around him. He was certainly putting up a fight and would always find someone to fight with or a reason to complain, and it seemed that method worked in keeping him alive. I cannot even believe how he survived the first incident of his illness in 2011, when I found him in a critical condition and rushed him to the hospital.

Luckily, he had a good circle of support to help him with everything from his grocery shopping to managing the house. It was mostly Ed Pastorini (amazing musician and one of the longest residents at Red Door), Jon Sadleir (Englishman and recent friend of Giorgio's), and myself.

Giorgio told me that he believed "the house" (Red Door) was possessed and protected by good and ancient spirits, and I am convinced that it was actually his very own spirit that had taken possession of the place. In May 2015, we did a final 'farewell to Red Door event' before the city shut it down and Giorgio was placed in an apartment. More importantly, the event was a living tribute to Giorgio, and we brought together many of his longtime friends and artists to perform in a multimedia 3D sculpture created for this living memorial.

This would be the last time Giorgio was at his house. Shortly afterward, I took Giorgio to the emergency room once again. This time he was admitted long-term to the hospital, and then to a nursing home in the Bronx, where he spent his last days. It was all complicated, frustrating, and sad to see how someone who had given so much to modern music and civilization was suddenly displaced and reduced to being accommodated at the only nursing home that would admit him. He wanted to pass his last days in the south of France, where his mother had been from and where he still had some distant family.

In early January 2016, I paid the last visit to Giorgio at the nursing home in the Bronx. I could sense that the end was very near and that I probably wouldn't see him again. I decided to play him a Yardbirds song from my phone, so I put the track "For Your Love" near his ear for him to hear. He vaguely nodded his head and gave me a sort of angry look as if to say, "Take that off!" Giorgio was always kind of shy about the things he did. So I then decided to play him a regional folk recording of "La Bamba," which is the most famous hymn from Veracruz, the Mexican port he once pictured retiring to. This time his face relaxed and seemed to be at peace. When the tune finished, I said, "Goodbye, Capitan," and left. A few hours later I received a call that Giorgio had passed.

As he started to get ill, shortly after his 75th birthday, he began having conversations with me about his dream to sell the house and retire in Mexico's port of Veracruz. He always lit up in a very sweet way when I talked to him about Veracruz, the "son jarocho" music from there, the coffee culture, and the old people dancing in the square to what is a combination of Cuban son and Mexican folk. I could see Giorgio dreamingly thinking about retiring in Veracruz in those late-night conversations we had.

I want to believe that it's where he is now."

– Raul Gonzalez

Raul Gonzalez sitting with guitar, 2015

Graffiti on the door of Giorgio's house at 140 West 24th St
on February 27th, 2016

15. ADIEU MAGUS

The writing of this biography has been therapeutic for me although it seems as if this book has written itself and that I was only its penholder. The man I had the privilege of knowing for 36 years – and being a close friend to for 10 years – was a force of nature. He was a man of mystery, perhaps because of his many experiences living in Georgia, the Middle East, Italy, Switzerland, England, France, and finally in New York, where he spent close to half of his life. How many times had he adapted to each of these new surroundings? How many times had he reinvented himself?

The colour of the entrance door to the house at 140 West 24th Street in Manhattan was the name he gave to the experimental music events he hosted there. They were the popular Green Door Parties, which then became the Red Door Parties. For years, celebrities of the international world of music did pass by, like Joe Strummer, Joey Ramone, Cheap Trick, Deborah Harry, Madonna, and many others.

But much more importantly, these music events were the breeding ground for a countless number of New York underground bands and musicians, like Jesse Malin and the D Generation, Jeff Buckley, Bad Brains, Nico, the Rapture, the Walkmen, Richard Hell (whom Giorgio used to fondly call Ricardo Inferno), Richard Lloyd, the Voidoids, Ed Pastorini and the 101 Crustaceans, and Band of Susans, as well as bands I managed such as the Volcanos and Surgery.

Six weeks after his passing, I walked by the house on February 27, 2016, the day before his birthday. All kinds of graffiti had been painted on the door, with messages of love and thanks. A bouquet of flowers was lying next to the door.

Above the handle, between the two orders to vacate, somebody had painted the following message: "In memorie Giorgio Gomelsky – 2/28/34 to 1/13/16 – May you soar with the Goddesses and inspire the stars!"

When Lilian and I passed by 140 West 24th Street on August 11, 2017, the house where he had lived for close to thirty-eight years, this den of the New York underground which so many of us had known and loved, was no more. The bulldozers were finishing razing it and later the Hyatt Place Hotel was constructed in its place.

Giorgio's love of life, his dynamism, and his creativity led him to push the envelope much further than anyone I know would have dared. But these same qualities were often misunderstood and underappreciated by those who were not in the music business for the music but for fame, glory or financial reward.

The bulldozers at 140 West 24th Street on August 11, 2017

The Hyatt Place Hotel at 140 West 24th Street today

Giorgio was more of an artist than a businessman. He became a manager and a producer because of his ability to enable others and his nose for the next coming thing, while initially he just wanted to produce and direct films. Although he had a talent for enabling others, in fact, he needed a manager just as much as they did. He did the best he could while preserving his own integrity on all occasions. If he was bitter, he did not show it, and until the end he kept his faith in the future, an attitude that always guided him.

More than anything, he was a great communicator who knew how to use all the means at his disposal to touch people around the world. He was a polymath who constantly drew from his deep bag of literary, cultural, and historic knowledge to sculpt the world he envisioned.

He wanted to educate, and he thought that knowledge should be made freely available to everybody and not be reserved for an elite. He believed in artistic freedom for all. This may be what motivated Eric Burdon to call Giorgio a "Mad Russian Intellectual" on the sleeve of his album *Winds of Change* in September 1967. Giorgio's goal was not so much to make money but rather to create events which would energise both the musicians and their audience to create a kind of symbiosis, a feedback loop of energy being transmitted from the band to their audience, a kind of zen feeling when everyone was in the groove.

The two most striking examples of this are the concept of the 'rave up,' which the Yardbirds heralded, and the Zu New Music Manifestival, where the 'Magus' Giorgio created the space and the opportunity for a gathering of incredible musicians from around the world. He simply guided the proceedings, backstage, like a grand wizard with a winning smile and sparkling eyes, encouraging those present to do more, to experiment, to break out of their comfort zones.

This desire to create exciting events was the constant thread of his life, from the very first concert of the Rolling Stones for an audience of three at the Crawdaddy, to the last Red Door Parties, which he continued to organize even though the City of New York was ordering him to vacate the premises. The root problem was that these magical experiences were not financially profitable. Giorgio used the money he received to create these unforgettable experiences but the musicians needed money, just like the record labels, and this was an endless source of conflict.

The most productive period of the Yardbirds commercially, the one that delivered the most hits on the UK and US hit parades, was undeniably the period when Giorgio managed and produced their records. In an interview that he gave Philippe Paringaux for *Rock & Folk* No. 42, Giorgio mentioned that Paul Samwell-Smith had said, "The biggest mistake we made was to break up with Giorgio," a separation that led to the band splitting up, even if it became the springboard for Jimmy Page to launch Led Zeppelin.

In the same vein, when we think now of Gong or Magma, we tend to recall their heyday in the 1970s, when

Giorgio was their producer/manager. Moreover, for an extraordinarily large number of New York musicians who struggled in the 1980s and 1990s to have their music heard against all odds, Giorgio's house, and his encouragement, provided many of us with a sense of direction.

Of course, Giorgio could be disappointing and irritating at times, and he grew agitated in his old age, but friendship is a two-way street and you learn to give and receive. First, I was a fan of the music he produced, but later I admired his ability to foster creativity in others. He shone as he illuminated the way for many great artists, who received the advice and encouragment they needed to make their dreams come true. His house was a place where anything could happen if the musicians would just push themselves artistically. He called his house a laboratory, and indeed, he mixed all the elements – arts, cultures, and people, like an alchemist trying to turn lead into gold, or turn the rough ashlar into spiritual matter – music being the key that elevates and transcends our spirit.

I think that Giorgio was the only person I ever met who perfectly incarnated the words of John Lennon in his utopian anthem "Imagine." It is worth noting that Giorgio lived only 48 blocks from the apartment where John Lennon lived with Yoko Ono, and where John was tragically assassinated on December 8, 1980.

Like the record label he founded in 1976 called Utopia, Giorgio was a knight of Planet Utopia, with his vision of an ideal world where everyone could live freely in their own way. He was always a big picture person, whose ideas were not always understood by the people around him, although they were sometimes prophetic. I hope that he has now found his own planet of peace, where music reigns and where "the train keeps a-rollin' all night long."

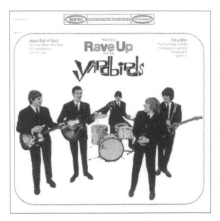

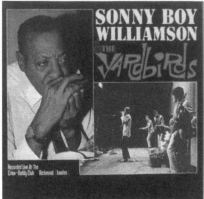

SUPERNOVA
BOOKS

50 Women in the Blues
Jennifer Noble & Zoë Howe
9781913641191   £19.99

The British Beat Explosion:
Rock 'n' Roll Island
Ed. JC Wheatley
9781906582470   £9.99

Women Make Noise: Girl Bands
from Motown to the Modern
Ed. Julia Downes
9780956632913   £15.99

On the Trail of Americana Music
Ralph Brookfield
9781913641092   £15.99

Rock's Diamond Year
Ralph Brookfield
9781913641221   £12.99

Pop Rock Icons: London's Swingin'
60s &70s
Philippe Margotin &
David Sinclair
9781913641269   £24.99

More great music books at
www.supernovabooks.co.uk